Sharing the Dharma

10-minute Dharma Talks for
American Zen Sanghas

by Min'ui Maitri

First Edition: June 2026
Published by One Dharma Zen, Tyler, Texas,
www.onedharmazen.org

CREDITS & ACKNOWLEDGMENTS
Cover and Interior Illustrations
Image credit: "Zen Monk Teaching in a Zendo" — AI-generated artwork created with Microsoft Copilot, 2026.
Photography: Photograph of "Min'ui Maitri - Bodhisattva Zen Priest" personal photo edited using Microsoft Copilot AI tools, under the direction of Min'ui Maitri, 2026.
Frontispiece family portrait at Mahabodhi Temple, Bodh Gaya, India, Family Archive, 2024.

Lineage Acknowledgments Liturgy and teaching frameworks adapted from the classical Zen expressions and include operational phrases of Zen Master Seung Sahn, with deep gratitude to the ancestral teachers of the Korean Seon tradition.

Library of Congress Cataloging-in-Publication Data
Maitri, Min'ui.
Sharing the Dharma: 10-Minute Dharma Talks for American Zen Sanghas / Min'ui Maitri.
Library of Congress Control Number: 2026913786
ISBN: 979-8-9963251-0-8 (paperback)
ISBN: 979-8-9963251-1-5 (Kindle)
Printed in the United States of America

Table of Contents

Introduction

This book is offered as a companion for practitioners, teachers, and sanghas seeking concise, accessible Dharma reflections rooted in an American Zen tradition. Each talk is designed to be brief enough for community use and clear enough to open reflection, discussion, and practice. Taken together, these pages explore foundational Buddhist teachings not as distant doctrines, but as living invitations to look directly at the nature of suffering, interdependence, compassion, emptiness, and awakening in everyday life.

The collection is arranged as a series of Dharma talk outlines followed by fuller talk texts, making it both practical and flexible. Readers may use it as a teaching resource, a study guide, or a devotional companion for personal practice. The aim throughout is not scholarly complexity for its own sake, but clarity in service of the path: language that can be spoken aloud in a zendo, received by a sangha, and carried back into the ordinary struggles and responsibilities of daily life.

Min'ui Maitri first encountered Buddhism in college in 1992 during a History of the Far East course. He was deeply moved by the promise of awakening and the cessation of suffering, though at the time non-attachment remained more concept than lived reality. Years later, after serving as a diplomat in Bali, Indonesia, and enduring depression and PTSD in the aftermath of the 2002 terrorist bombings, he turned to meditation in search of relief from intense mental suffering. That search first led him through the teachings of Pure Land then Theravada Buddhism, and eventually, in 2010, to Zen. Through Zen practice, he found a path of healing, stability, and direct transformation.

Traveling along this Zen path, he was ordained as a Novice Zen Priest in 2017, reaffirmed those vows in 2021, and as a Bodhisattva Zen Priest in 2023. In 2024, he made pilgrimage to

Bodh Gaya, India, to visit the great Bodhi Tree beneath which the Buddha Gotama awakened. His studies continue each day, not as a finished attainment but as an ongoing vow. Like all Bodhisattvas, he responds whenever he can to opportunities to share the Dharma. He currently resides with his family in Da Nang, Vietnam, where practice and teaching remain inseparable from the rhythms of daily life.

These talks arise from that lived journey: from study, suffering, practice, devotion, and the wish to make the teachings usable for others. They are meant to encourage reflection without pretense, discipline without rigidity, and compassion without sentimentality. If they help even one reader or one sangha meet the Dharma more intimately, then this offering has served its purpose.

Min'ui and family at Mahabodhi Temple, Bodh Gaya, India, 2024.

PART 1 - Foundations of the Path

Dharma Talk Outline: The Life of Buddha Gotama

1. Opening Frame (1–2 minutes)

- Present the Buddha not as a supernatural figure, but as a human being who discovered something profound about the nature of suffering and freedom.
- Emphasize: **"The Buddha's life is our life — the same fears, the same longings, the same potential."**
- The story is not history for history's sake; it's a map of the spiritual journey.

2. Birth and Early Life (1–2 minutes)

A. Birth in Lumbini
- Born as Siddhartha Gotama to Queen Māyā and King Suddhodana.
- Queen Māyā's dream and the auspicious signs symbolize **potential**, not destiny.

B. Raised in Luxury
- Sheltered from sickness, aging, and death.
- His father tries to protect him from anything unpleasant — a metaphor for **our own avoidance of discomfort**.
-

Teaching Point
Sheltering ourselves from suffering does not prevent suffering — it only delays wisdom.

3. The Four Sights (2–3 minutes)

This is the turning point.
1. **Old Age**
2. **Sickness**
3. **Death**
4. **A wandering ascetic**

- These sights shatter his protected worldview.
- He realizes: **"No amount of comfort can protect me from impermanence."**

Teaching Point

The Four Sights represent the moment we stop pretending life is something other than what it is.

4. The Great Renunciation (1–2 minutes)

- At age 29, Siddhartha leaves the palace, his wealth, his status, and even his newborn son.
- Not out of rejection, but out of **urgency** — the desire to understand suffering.
- This is the archetype of stepping onto the path.

Teaching Point

Every spiritual journey begins with letting go of illusions.

5. The Six Years of Asceticism (2–3 minutes)

A. Extreme Practices
- Fasting, breath-holding, self-mortification.
- Becomes so emaciated he nearly dies.

B. Realization
- Asceticism is just another form of clinging — clinging to purity, achievement, spiritual pride.

C. Sujātā's Offering
- A village woman offers him milk-rice.
- This restores his strength and inspires the **Middle Way**.

Teaching Point

Wisdom often comes not from extremes, but from balance and humility.

6. Awakening Under the Bodhi Tree (2–3 minutes)

A. The Night of Awakening
- Faces Māra — fear, desire, doubt.
- Touches the earth as witness.

B. Insight
- Sees dependent arising clearly.
- Understands the nature of suffering and its cessation.
- Realizes the freedom of non-self and compassion.

C. Becomes the Buddha
- "The Awakened One," not "the Enlightened One."

Teaching Point
Awakening is not escaping the world — it's seeing the world without distortion.

7. Teaching for 45 Years (2–3 minutes)

A. First Turning of the Wheel
- Teaches the Four Noble Truths and the Eightfold Path.

B. Establishes the Sangha
- Monks, nuns, laypeople — a community of practice.

C. Radical Inclusivity
- Teaches kings and beggars, murderers and merchants, men and women.
- Mahāpajāpatī becomes the first bhikkhunī.

Teaching Point
The Dharma is for everyone — no one is excluded from awakening.

8. Final Days and Parinirvāṇa (1–2 minutes)

A. Last Teaching
- "All conditioned things are impermanent. Strive on with diligence."

B. Passing at Kusinagara

- Not a tragedy — a reminder of the naturalness of impermanence.

Teaching Point

The Buddha's death is part of his teaching: nothing is fixed, nothing is final, everything is practice.

9. Closing (1 minute)

- Bring it home: **"The Buddha's life is not a story about a special man — it's a story about what is possible for all of us."**
- Invite practitioners to reflect on which part of the Buddha's journey mirrors their own right now.
- End with: **"Awakening is not far away — it is as close as your next breath."**

The Life of Buddha Gotama: A Map of Our Own Journey

When we study the life of the historical Buddha, it is easy to get caught up in the mythic, miraculous elements of the narrative. In our practice, however, we reframe his story entirely, viewing him not as a remote, supernatural deity, but as a human being who discovered something profoundly liberating about the nature of suffering. The Buddha's life is ultimately a mirror of our own lives, containing the very same fears, the exact same longings, and the identical spiritual potential. His biography is not history for history's sake; it is a living map of our collective spiritual journey.

The story begins in Lumbini with the birth of Siddhartha Gotama to Queen Māyā and King Suddhodana. Raised in the absolute height of royal luxury, the young prince was aggressively sheltered from the painful realities of sickness, aging, and death. His father went to extreme lengths to ensure Siddhartha never encountered anything unpleasant, creating an artificial environment of perpetual pleasure. This royal bubble serves as a perfect metaphor for our own modern lives, where we constantly build walls of comfort to avoid psychological discomfort. Sheltering ourselves from the reality of suffering does not prevent it, however, and it only serves to delay the onset of true wisdom.

The inevitable turning point arrived when the prince stepped outside the palace gates and encountered the famous Four Sights: an old man, a sick person, a corpse, and finally, a peaceful, wandering ascetic. These sights completely shattered his protected worldview, forcing him to realize that no amount of wealth or privilege could ever protect him from the law of impermanence. The Four Sights represent the exact moment in our own lives when we stop pretending. They mark the courageous transition where we refuse to look away from reality exactly as it is.

Driven by a profound sense of existential urgency, Siddhartha made the radical decision at age twenty-nine to leave the palace, abandoning his wealth, status, and family. This act, known as the Great Renunciation, was not born out of a cold rejection of the world, but out of an urgent need to understand the root cause of human sorrow. This is the timeless archetype of stepping onto the spiritual path. Every genuine spiritual journey must begin with this same willingness to let go of our comfortable, familiar illusions.

The Pendulum of Experience

Siddhartha's path to awakening demonstrates the futility of chasing extreme states of mind or body:

- **The Palace:** A life of total indulgence that numbs the mind and obscures the truth of change.
- **The Forest:** Six years of extreme self-mortification that leaves him emaciated and near death, revealing that spiritual pride and asceticism are just alternative forms of clinging.
- **The Middle Way:** Inspired by Sujātā's timely offering of simple milk-rice, he discovers that true clarity emerges only from a foundation of balance, care, and basic humility.

This newfound balance led him directly to the base of the Bodhi tree, where he vowed to sit until he uncovered the truth. Throughout the night of his awakening, Siddhartha faced down the psychological assaults of Māra, representing his own deepest internal fears, desires, and lingering doubts. He did not engage in conflict with these shadows; instead, he touched the earth to witness his right to occupy that space.

As the morning star rose, he saw the mechanism of dependent arising with absolute clarity, transforming completely into the Buddha. It is worth noting that the title *Buddha* means "The Awakened One," not "The Enlightened One." Awakening is not an exotic escape from our world into a celestial cloud; it is the simple, radical act of seeing the world exactly as it is, entirely free from the distortions of the ego.

The Buddha spent the next forty-five years walking the dusty roads of India, turning the wheel of the Dharma by teaching the Four Noble Truths and the Eightfold Path. He established the *Sangha*—a community of practice composed of monks, nuns, and laypeople. His teaching style was characterized by a radical inclusivity that shattered the rigid caste system of his era. He taught kings and beggars, murderers and merchants, men and women alike, eventually ordaining his own stepmother, Mahāpajāpatī, as the first Buddhist nun. The Dharma was, and remains, completely universal, leaving no single human being excluded from the possibility of freedom.

Even the Buddha's final days at Kusinagara serve as a profound teaching. Passing away at the age of eighty, his final words to his grieving disciples were direct: *"All conditioned things are impermanent. Strive on with diligence."* His death was not a tragedy, but a final demonstration of the naturalness of change.

The Buddha's life is not a story about an untouchable, special man who lived in the distant past. It is a blueprint of what is possible for you and me. We can pause today and reflect on which part of his journey mirrors our own current life situation, whether we are suffocating in a palace of comfort, struggling in a forest of effort, or finally preparing to sit down under our own tree of awakening. This freedom is never far away; it is as close as your very next breath.

Dharma Talk Outline: The Four Noble Truths

1. Opening Frame (1–2 minutes)

- Present the Four Noble Truths as **diagnosis and cure**, not dogma.
- Emphasize: **"The Buddha wasn't teaching pessimism. He was teaching realism — and the path to freedom."**
- These truths are not beliefs; they are **observations** anyone can verify in their own life.

2. First Noble Truth — Dukkha: The Truth of Suffering (2–3 minutes)

A. What Dukkha Really Means

- Not just "suffering," but:
  - Unsatisfactoriness
  - Stress
  - The feeling that something is always slightly off
- Even pleasant experiences contain dukkha because they are impermanent.

B. Three Types of Dukkha
1. **Ordinary suffering** — pain, loss, illness.
2. **Suffering of change** — good things don't last.
3. **Suffering of conditioned existence** — the subtle tension of being a self.

Teaching Point
The Buddha begins with honesty: life is unstable, unpredictable, and often painful — and pretending otherwise only increases suffering.

3. Second Noble Truth — Samudaya: The Cause of Suffering (2–3 minutes)

A. The Cause Is Craving (Tanhā)

- Grasping for what we want
- Pushing away what we don't want
- Ignoring what we don't understand

B. Three Forms of Craving

1. **Craving for sense pleasure**
2. **Craving for becoming** (identity, status, self-image)
3. **Craving for non-becoming** (escape, numbness, annihilation)

C. The Psychological Insight

Craving is not the same as desire. Craving is **desire + clinging + identity**.
Teaching Point
Suffering doesn't come from life — it comes from the way we cling to life.

4. Third Noble Truth — Nirodha: The Cessation of Suffering (2–3 minutes)

A. The Heart of the Teaching

If craving ends, suffering ends.

B. What Cessation Is Not

- Not annihilation
- Not apathy
- Not withdrawal from life

C. What Cessation *Is*

- Freedom from compulsive reactivity
- Peace in the midst of change
- The taste of non-clinging
- The realization of emptiness and interdependence

Teaching Point
Nirodha is not a mystical state — it's the moment you stop fighting reality.

5. Fourth Noble Truth — Magga: The Path (2–3 minutes)

A. The Eightfold Path
1. Right View
2. Right Intention
3. Right Speech
4. Right Action
5. Right Livelihood
6. Right Effort
7. Right Mindfulness
8. Right Concentration

B. Three Groupings
- **Wisdom** (1–2)
- **Ethics** (3–5)
- **Meditation** (6–8)

C. The Middle Way
- Avoiding extremes of indulgence and asceticism.
- A path of balance, clarity, and compassion.

Teaching Point
The Path is not a ladder — it's a way of living with awareness and kindness.

6. The Zen Angle (1–2 minutes)
- Zen emphasizes that the Four Noble Truths are not philosophical positions — they are **immediate experiences**.
- In zazen:
    - We see dukkha directly.
    - We see craving arise and fall.
    - We taste moments of cessation.
    - We walk the path simply by sitting.

Zen expression
"Nothing to add, nothing to remove."

7. Closing (1 minute)

- Bring it home: **"The Four Noble Truths are not ancient teachings — they are the story of every moment of our lives."**
- Invite practitioners to notice one moment today where craving arises, and simply soften around it.
- End with: **"Suffering is not a failure — it is the beginning of wisdom."**

The Four Noble Truths: Diagnosis and Cure for Everyday Life

The Four Noble Truths form the absolute cornerstone of the Buddhist tradition, yet they are frequently misinterpreted as a gloomy, pessimistic philosophy. When the Buddha delivered these insights, however, he was not teaching pessimism; he was teaching radical realism, offering a clear diagnosis and a reliable cure for human discontent. These truths are not dogmatic religious beliefs that demand blind faith. They are practical observations about the mechanics of the human mind, open for anyone to test, investigate, and verify within their own lived experience.

The journey begins with the First Noble Truth, the reality of **dukkha**. While traditionally translated simply as "suffering," the term carries a much subtler psychological weight. It points to a chronic sense of unsatisfactoriness, stress, and the lingering background feeling that something in our lives is always slightly off. Even our most joyful, pleasant experiences contain an element of *dukkha* because they are inherently impermanent. The tradition structures this reality into three distinct layers:

- **Ordinary suffering:** The obvious physical and emotional pain of loss, aging, heartbreak, and illness.
- **The suffering of change:** The anxiety that arises because the good things in our lives cannot last forever.
- **The suffering of conditioned existence:** The deep, subtle tension of trying to maintain a solid, permanent ego-identity in a completely fluid universe.

The Buddha begins his teaching with absolute honesty, reminding us that life is unstable, unpredictable, and often painful. Pretending otherwise only serves to increase our underlying suffering.

Once the diagnosis is established, the Second Noble Truth uncovers the cause of this discontent: **samudaya**, which is craving (*taṇhā*). This craving is the frantic, instinctual mechanism of grasping for what we want, pushing away what we do not want, and ignoring what we do not understand. It manifests through three specific forms: the craving for sensory pleasure, the craving for becoming an idealized identity or status, and the craving for non-becoming, which is the urge to escape, numb out, or annihilate our awareness. There is a vital psychological distinction to make here: suffering does not arise from simple human desire. Suffering is born only when desire is coupled with tight clinging and a defensive sense of identity. It does not come from life itself; it comes from the desperate way we grip onto life.

The Medical Analogy

The Four Noble Truths operate exactly like an ancient medical protocol, treating the psychological illness of human reactivity:

- **The Diagnosis (*Dukkha*):** Identifying the symptom of chronic unsatisfactoriness and unrest.
- **The Cause (*Samudaya*):** Pinpointing the root infection, which is our deep-seated habit of craving and clinging.
- **The Cure (*Nirodha*):** Recognizing that health is possible, and that suffering ceases when craving is released.
- **The Treatment (*Magga*):** Implementing the specific, daily prescription of the Noble Eightfold Path.

The Third Noble Truth, *nirodha*, offers the radical promise of a cure: if craving ends, suffering ends. This cessation is not a state of cold, apathetic withdrawal from the world, nor is it the literal annihilation of our personality. Cessation is simply the complete freedom from compulsive reactivity. It is the ability to maintain deep inner peace right in the midst of chaotic change, touching the transformative taste of non-clinging. This is the direct realization of emptiness and interdependence. *Nirodha* is never an exotic, mystical state of consciousness reserved for saints; it is the ordinary, quiet moment when you finally stop fighting reality exactly as it presents itself.

The treatment plan is laid out in the Fourth Noble Truth, **magga**, which is the Noble Eightfold Path. This comprehensive blueprint represents the Middle Way, carefully avoiding the twin extremes of sensory indulgence and harsh, aggressive asceticism. The path is divided into three natural training groupings:

1. **Wisdom:** Cultivating Right View and Right Intention to orient our understanding.
2. **Ethics:** Embodying Right Speech, Right Action, and Right Livelihood to stabilize our relationships.
3. **Meditation:** Developing Right Effort, Right Mindfulness, and Right Concentration to steady the mind.

This path is not a linear ladder where we climb past earlier steps; it is an integrated, beautiful way of living through constant awareness and kindness.

In our Zen tradition, we emphasize that these Four Noble Truths are not abstract philosophical positions to argue about. They are immediate experiences to be witnessed directly on the meditation cushion. In the stillness of zazen, we see *dukkha* as our legs ache or our minds drift. We watch craving arise and fall like waves when a distraction enters our awareness. We taste brief, beautiful moments of complete cessation whenever a thought dissolves into nothingness, walking the entire path simply by remaining still. A classic Zen expression captures this effortless alignment: *"Nothing to add, nothing to remove."*

The Four Noble Truths are not an ancient historical text; they are the living story of every single moment of our lives. When we meet a difficult situation today, we can choose to notice the exact moment craving arises, and simply soften our physical and mental grip around it. Suffering is never a personal failure or a sign of spiritual defeat. It is the necessary, fertile soil where the seeds of wisdom begin to take root.

Dharma Talk Outline: The Noble Eightfold Path (VISALEMC)

"When traveling through samsara, you need your VISA LEt eM C(see)."

1. Opening Frame (1–2 minutes)
- Present the Eightfold Path as the **practical heart** of the Buddha's teaching.
- Emphasize: **It's not eight commandments — it's eight aspects of a single integrated way of living.**
- Introduce your mnemonic: **VISALEMC — the passport for traveling through samsara.**

2. V — Right View (1–2 minutes)

What it means
Seeing reality clearly: impermanence, interdependence, non-self, and the nature of suffering.
Why it matters
Right View is the compass — without it, the rest of the path wanders.
Practice angle
Notice when you're believing a story instead of seeing what's actually happening.

3. I — Right Intention (1–2 minutes)

What it means
Three intentions:
- Renunciation (letting go)
- Goodwill
- Harmlessness

Why it matters
Intention shapes karma more than action alone.
Practice angle
Ask: *"What is my heart doing right now?"*

4. S — Right Speech (1–2 minutes)

What it means
Speech that is truthful, kind, timely, and beneficial.
Why it matters
Speech creates worlds — relationships, trust, conflict, healing.
Practice angle
Pause before speaking. Is it true? Is it helpful? Is it necessary?

5. A — Right Action (1–2 minutes)

What it means
Ethical conduct:
- Not harming
- Not stealing
- Not misusing sexuality

Why it matters
Ethics is not morality — it's **non-harm** as a foundation for clarity.
Practice angle
Act in ways that leave no trace of regret.

6. L — Right Livelihood (1–2 minutes)

What it means
Work that does not harm others or yourself.
Why it matters
We spend most of our lives working — livelihood shapes the heart.
Practice angle
Ask: *"Does my work support awakening or obscure it?"*

7. E — Right Effort (1–2 minutes)

What it means
Four efforts:
- Prevent unwholesome states
- Abandon unwholesome states
- Cultivate wholesome states
- Maintain wholesome states

Why it matters
Effort is not strain — it's **joyful discipline**.
Practice angle
Lean toward what opens the heart; lean away from what closes it.

8. M — Right Mindfulness (2 minutes)

What it means
Clear awareness of body, feelings, mind, and phenomena.
Why it matters
Mindfulness is the thread that ties the whole path together.
Practice angle
Be intimate with your experience — not judging, just knowing.

9. C — Right Concentration (1–2 minutes)

What it means
Stable, collected, unified attention — the jhānic mind.
Why it matters
A concentrated mind sees deeply and responds wisely.
Practice angle
In zazen, allow the mind to settle into stillness without forcing.

10. The Path as a Whole (1–2 minutes)

- The Eightfold Path is **not linear** — it's a mandala.
- Each aspect supports the others.
- Ethics stabilizes the mind.
- Concentration deepens insight.
- Insight strengthens ethics.
- The whole thing spirals upward.

Zen expression
"Not eight steps — one path with eight facets."

11. Closing (1 minute)

- Bring it home: **"VISALEMC is not a list to memorize — it's a way to walk through the world with clarity and compassion."**
- Invite practitioners to choose one aspect to emphasize today.
- End with: **"This path is noble because it leads to freedom."**

The Noble Eightfold Path: Traveling Through Samsara

The Noble Eightfold Path is often presented as the practical heart of the Buddha's teaching. Rather than a set of rigid commandments, these eight steps represent an integrated, holistic way of living. To help practitioners navigate this vast territory, we can use a simple memory device: VISALEMC. Think of it as your passport for traveling through *samsara*, the endless cycle of reactive habit patterns. When traveling through *samsara*, you need your VISA to help you see clearly. This mnemonic guides us through eight distinct facets of a single, unified path.

The path begins with **Right View**, the *V* in our framework. Right View means seeing reality exactly as it is, recognizing the truth of impermanence, interdependence, non-self, and the nature of suffering. It serves as our compass. Without this foundational understanding, the rest of our practice easily wanders into confusion. In daily life, we practice Right View by noticing when we are buying into a fabricated personal story instead of observing what is actually happening in the present moment.

From clear vision arises **Right Intention**, the *I* of the path. This aspect focuses on three specific qualities of the heart: renunciation, goodwill, and harmlessness. Because our intentions shape our *karma* far more than outer actions alone, this inner orientation is vital. We practice Right View and Right Intention together by frequently pausing to ask ourselves a simple question: "What is my heart doing right now?"

Our inner intentions naturally manifest through **Right Speech**, the *S* of the acronym. This means cultivating speech that is truthful, kind, timely, and beneficial. Words create worlds, shaping our relationships, building trust, or triggering conflict. The practice here requires a deliberate pause before speaking to evaluate our words: Are they true? Are they helpful? Are they necessary?

When speech aligns with clarity, **Right Action** follows as the A in our passport. Right Action forms the basis of ethical conduct, traditionally defined as refraining from harming, stealing, and misusing sexuality. Within the Buddhist tradition, ethics is not about dogmatic morality; it is a practical foundation for mental clarity. We practice Right Action by moving through the world in ways that leave no lingering trace of regret.

Because we spend the majority of our waking hours working, **Right Livelihood**—the L—is indispensable. This facet means engaging in work that does not cause harm to ourselves or others. Our daily employment deeply shapes the heart, either clouding our awareness or refining it. A practitioner must honestly look at their career and ask: "Does my work support awakening, or does it obscure it?"

Sustaining this lifestyle requires **Right Effort**, the E in our framework. Right Effort consists of four specific practices: preventing unwholesome states, abandoning unwholesome states, cultivating wholesome states, and maintaining those wholesome states. Effort in this context does not mean tense strain; it is a joyful, steady discipline. We practice this by consistently leaning toward actions that open the heart and gently leaning away from those that close it.

The entire path is held together by **Right Mindfulness**, the M of VISALEMC. Right Mindfulness is the clear, non-judgmental awareness of the body, feelings, mind, and phenomena. It acts as the thread tying all eight aspects into a single garment. To embody this, we practice intimacy with our immediate experience, knowing what is happening while resisting the urge to criticize or judge it.

Finally, the path culminates in **Right Concentration**, the C that allows us to see. This is the cultivation of a stable, collected, and unified mind. A concentrated mind sees deeply into the nature of existence and responds with natural wisdom rather than knee-jerk reactivity. In our formal meditation, we practice Right

Concentration by allowing the mind to settle into stillness without forcing or gripping.

The Integrated Mandala

The Noble Eightfold Path is not a linear ladder; it is a dynamic mandala where every part feeds into the whole:

- **Ethics (Speech, Action, Livelihood)** stabilizes the mind and prevents regret.
- **Concentration (Effort, Mindfulness, Concentration)** deepens inner stillness.
- **Wisdom (View, Intention)** arises from stillness and strengthens our ethics.

This path is not a series of eight separate steps. It is one single path with eight beautiful facets, spiraling upward as we walk it. VISALEMC is not a checklist to memorize for an exam; it is a practical way to walk through a chaotic world with clarity and compassion. We can choose just one aspect to emphasize in our behavior today, trusting that a single step alters the entire journey. This path is called noble for a very simple reason: it leads directly to freedom.

PART 2 - The Anatomy of Experience

Dharma Talk Outline: The Six Senses, Sense Consciousnesses, and Dusts

1. Opening Frame (1–2 minutes)

- Begin by situating the teaching: *"In Zen, awakening isn't somewhere else — it's right here in our moment-to-moment contact with the world."*
- Introduce the classical Buddhist model: **Six sense bases → Six sense objects ("dusts") → Six consciousnesses.**
- Emphasize the practical point: *"This is a map of how experience forms — and how delusion forms — in real time."*

2. The Structure of Experience (2–3 minutes)

A. The Six Sense Bases
1. Eye
2. Ear
3. Nose
4. Tongue
5. Body
6. Mind (the sixth sense)

B. The Six Dusts
1. Form
2. Sound
3. Smell
4. Taste
5. Touch
6. Thoughts / mental objects

C. The Six Consciousnesses
- Each sense base + dust gives rise to a corresponding consciousness.
- Example: eye + form → eye-consciousness.

Teaching point: **Experience is not "out there" or "in here." It arises in the meeting.**

3. Why "Dusts"? (1–2 minutes)

- The word "dust" suggests:
    o Impermanence
    o Insignificance
    o The way things cling to us and obscure clarity
- The senses themselves are not the problem — **it's the sticking**.
- Zen metaphor: *"The mirror is originally clear; dust only settles when we stop paying attention."*

4. How Delusion Forms (3–4 minutes)

Walk through the chain in a relatable way:
1. Contact
- A sound, a sight, a thought appears.
2. Feeling Tone (Vedana)
- Pleasant, unpleasant, or neutral.
3. Reaction
- Craving, aversion, or ignorance.
4. Proliferation (Papanca)
- The mind builds stories, identities, fears, hopes.

Teaching point: **The senses are innocent. The trouble begins when consciousness grasps.**

Use a simple example:
- Hearing a notification ding → pleasant anticipation → reaching → checking → spiraling into distraction.

Or:
- A thought arises: "I'm not doing enough." The dust is the thought; the suffering is the clinging.

5. The Zen Approach: Returning to Direct Experience (3–4 minutes)

A. Mindfulness of the Senses

- Practice is not shutting down the senses but meeting them clearly.
- "Just seeing, just hearing, just thinking."

B. The Sixth Sense: Mind
- Thoughts are treated like any other sense object.
- This is liberating: *"A thought is just a thought — not a command, not a truth."*

C. Non-attachment
- We don't polish the mirror to make it shiny; we polish it to see clearly.
- The dust will always return — the practice is simply noticing.

D. The Moment of Freedom
- Freedom appears **at the moment of contact**, before reaction.
- This is the heart of Zen: *"Right here, in this seeing, hearing, touching — the Dharma is alive."*

6. Closing (1 minute)

- Invite practitioners to notice one sense experience right now.
- Ask: *"Can you meet this sound, this breath, this thought without adding anything?"*
- End with the reminder: **When we see the dust clearly, it no longer obscures the mirror.**

The Six Senses, Sense Consciousnesses, and Dusts

In the Zen tradition, we often remind ourselves that awakening is not located in some far-off, exotic realm. It is found right here, in our moment-to-moment contact with the world. To help us navigate this immediate reality, classical Buddhism provides a precise structural model: six sense bases, six sense objects, and six corresponding consciousnesses. This framework is not an academic theory; it is a real-time map showing exactly how human experience forms, and how delusion takes root, in every waking second.

To understand this map, we must examine the interlocking components that create our sensory world.

- **The Six Sense Bases**: The eye, ear, nose, tongue, body, and the mind itself, which Buddhism treats as the sixth sense organ.
- **The Six Sense Objects**: Form, sound, smell, taste, touch, and thoughts or mental objects.
- **The Six Consciousnesses**: The specific awareness that arises when a sense base meets a sense object, such as eye-consciousness or ear-consciousness.

Experience does not exist independently "out there" in the world, nor does it exist isolated "in here" within our heads. It arises dynamically in the exact moment of their meeting.

The traditional term for the objects of our senses is "dusts," a word chosen with deep intent. Dust suggests impermanence, insignificance, and the subtle way worldly things cling to us and obscure our innate clarity. The senses themselves are entirely innocent; the problem lies in our tendency to stick to what we perceive. A classic Zen metaphor reminds us that the mirror of the mind is originally clear, and dust only settles when we stop paying attention.

The Anatomy of a Sensory Spiral

Delusion forms through a predictable, lightning-fast chain reaction. Consider how a simple notification sound traps the mind:

- **Contact:** The ear base meets the sound object, triggering ear-consciousness.
- **Feeling Tone:** The mind instantly registers the sound with a pleasant flavor.
- **Reaction:** An instinctive craving arises, urging us to grab the phone.
- **Mental Proliferation:** The mind spins into a story, anticipating a message, checking alerts, and spiraling into total distraction.

This same process applies to our internal world. A thought arises in the mind: *"I am not doing enough."* In this framework, the thought is simply dust passing across the sixth sense base. The suffering does not belong to the thought itself; the suffering is born from our automatic habit of grasping onto it.

The Zen approach to this sensory machinery is not to shut down our senses or retreat from the world. True practice means meeting our senses clearly, practicing what the teachings call "just seeing, just hearing, just thinking." We treat our thoughts exactly like sounds or smells—as passing phenomena rather than absolute commands or ultimate truths. This shift in perspective is profoundly liberating.

We do not polish the mirror of the mind to keep it perpetually sterile, because the dust of life will always return. Our practice is simply to notice the dust without attachment. True spiritual freedom appears at the very moment of sensory contact, right before our habitual reaction kicks in. Right here, in this immediate seeing, hearing, and touching, the Dharma is completely alive. As we will see when we map the twelve-link chain of experience, this moment of contact is the precise intersection where our automatic conditioning can either ignite a lifetime of habit or dissolve into immediate spaciousness.

We can practice this direct meeting by bringing awareness to our immediate surroundings. Notice one single sensory experience occurring right now—a distant sound, the weight of your breath, or a passing thought. Try to meet this experience cleanly, without adding a single story, judgment, or preference to it. When we see the dust clearly for what it is, it loses its power to obscure the mirror.

Dharma Talk Outline: The Five Skandhas — Understanding the Self as Process

1. Opening Frame (1–2 minutes)

- Introduce the Skandhas as the Buddha's analysis of what we call "self."
- Emphasize: **"The Five Skandhas show that the self is not a thing — it's an ongoing activity."**
- They are not metaphysical categories; they are **moment-to-moment experiences**.

2. The Five Skandhas in Order (2–3 minutes)

Give the list cleanly first:
1. **Form (Rūpa)**
2. **Feeling Tone (Vedanā)**
3. **Perception (Saṃjñā)**
4. **Mental Formations (Saṃskāra)**
5. **Consciousness (Vijñāna)**

Teaching point: **These five together create the illusion of a solid "I."**

3. Skandha One — Form (Rūpa) (1–2 minutes)

What it is
- The physical body
- The senses
- The material world

Symbolic meaning
- Impermanence
- Vulnerability
- Embodiment

Practice angle

Notice the body as changing sensations, not a fixed identity.

4. Skandha Two — Feeling Tone (Vedanā) (1–2 minutes)

What it is
- The immediate flavor of experience:
  - Pleasant
  - Unpleasant
  - Neutral

Why it matters
- Feeling tone is the spark that ignites craving and aversion.

Practice angle

Catch the feeling tone before the story forms.

5. Skandha Three — Perception (Saṃjñā) (1–2 minutes)

What it is
- Labeling, recognizing, categorizing.
- Turning raw sensation into "something."

Why it matters
- Perception is fast and often inaccurate.
- It creates the world of "this is good," "this is bad," "this is me."

Practice angle

Notice how quickly the mind names things — and how freeing it is to let the labels soften.

6. Skandha Four — Mental Formations (Saṃskāra) (2–3 minutes)

What it is
- Thoughts
- Emotions
- Habits
- Intentions
- Conditioning
- Karma

Why it matters
- This is where most of our suffering lives.
- These formations are not "you" — they are **patterns arising from causes and conditions**.

Practice angle

See thoughts and emotions as weather patterns, not identity.

7. Skandha Five — Consciousness (Vijñāna) (1–2 minutes)

What it is
- Awareness tied to each sense base
- Not a permanent soul
- A stream, not a container

Why it matters
- Consciousness depends on the other four Skandhas — it is not independent.

Practice angle
Rest in awareness itself — spacious, fluid, not owned by a self.

8. The Skandhas as a Process, Not a Person (1–2 minutes)

- The Buddha's insight: **There is no "self" behind the Skandhas — the Skandhas *are* what we call self.**
- They arise together, change together, and dissolve together.
- This is the heart of non-self (anattā).

Zen expression
"No fixed self to defend, no fixed self to improve."

9. Why Understanding the Skandhas Is Liberating (2–3 minutes)

A. Reduces clinging
If there's no solid self, there's nothing to protect.

B. Softens reactivity
We see emotions as passing formations, not personal failures.

C. Opens compassion
Others are also just Skandhas in motion — not enemies, not obstacles.

D. Reveals emptiness

Each Skandha is dependently arisen, therefore empty of fixed essence.

E. Supports zazen

In sitting, we watch the Skandhas arise and fall — and discover spaciousness.

10. Closing (1 minute)

- Bring it home: **"The Five Skandhas show us that the self is not a thing — it's a dance."**
- Invite practitioners to notice one Skandha today as it arises.
- End with: **"When we stop clinging to the Skandhas, the world opens."**

The Five Skandhas: Understanding the Self as Process

The Buddha offered a radical analysis of what we conventionally call the "self" through a framework known as the Five Skandhas. These aggregates show us that the self is not a static thing; it is an ongoing, dynamic activity. Rather than serving as abstract metaphysical categories, the skandhas describe our moment-to-moment human experience. By examining them closely, we discover that what we mistake for a solid, unchanging identity is actually a collection of fluid processes.

To study this mechanism, we must first look at the five components in their natural order of operation.

1. **Form** (*Rūpa*)
2. **Feeling Tone** (*Vedanā*)
3. **Perception** (*Saṃjñā*)
4. **Mental Formations** (*Saṃskāra*)
5. **Consciousness** (*Vijñāna*)

Working together in rapid succession, these five aggregates create the powerful illusion of a solid, independent "I."

The process begins with the first skandha, **Form**, which encompasses our physical body, our sense organs, and the material world. Form represents our embodiment, carrying with it the inherent traits of impermanence and vulnerability. In our meditation practice, we learn to investigate this physical aspect directly. Instead of viewing the body as a fixed identity that belongs to us, we begin to notice it as a shifting constellation of changing sensations.

The moment form interacts with the world, the second skandha arises: **Feeling Tone**. This is the immediate, instinctual flavor of any given experience, categorized simply as pleasant, unpleasant, or neutral. Feeling tone is the crucial spark that ignites our psychological habits of craving and aversion. If a sensation is pleasant, we want to grab it; if it is unpleasant, we want to push it away. A practitioner targets this specific link in the chain, learning to catch the raw feeling tone before the mind spins a dramatic story around it.

Close on the heels of feeling tone comes the third skandha, **Perception**. This is the faculty of labeling, recognizing, and categorizing raw data. Perception turns a generic auditory frequency into "a car horn" or a visual pattern into "a friend." This process happens incredibly fast and is often inaccurate, yet it constructs our entire subjective world of preferences. We practice with perception by noticing how quickly the mind names things, discovering the immense freedom that comes when we let those rigid labels soften.

The fourth skandha, **Mental Formations**, is the vast realm where thoughts, emotions, habits, intentions, and conditioned responses live. This aggregate is the storehouse of our *karma*, and it is where the majority of our psychological suffering resides. We frequently mistake these deep-seated habits for our actual identity. These formations are not "you" at all; they are merely psychological patterns arising from specific causes and conditions. On the cushion, we practice seeing our thoughts and emotions as passing weather patterns rather than the sky itself.

The final component is the fifth skandha, **Consciousness**. This is the bare awareness tied to each of our sense bases, such as eye-consciousness or ear-consciousness. It is vital to understand that consciousness is not a permanent soul or a static container. It is a flowing stream that depends entirely on the other four skandhas to exist. In our practice, we learn to rest in this spacious, fluid awareness without trying to possess or own it.

The Anatomy of an Experience

To see how the skandhas create the illusion of a self in real-time, consider a single moment:

- **Form:** An auditory wave hits the eardrum (sound meets the ear).

- **Feeling Tone:** The mind instantly registers the sound as unpleasant.
- **Perception:** The mind identifies the sound: *"That is my neighbor's leaf blower."*
- **Mental Formations:** Irritation arises, followed by a thought: *"They always ruin my morning."*
- **Consciousness:** The bare awareness of this entire shifting sequence.

The Buddha's insight reveals that there is no hidden "self" pulling the strings behind these stages. The skandhas themselves *are* what we call the self. They arise together, change together, and dissolve together, forming the core of the teaching on non-self (*anattā*). In the Zen tradition, we express this truth by recognizing that there is no fixed self to defend, and no fixed self to improve.

Understanding the skandhas in this way is profoundly liberating for our daily life. It naturally reduces our clinging; if there is no solid ego at the center of our lives, we realize there is nothing we need to protect. This insight softens our reactivity, allowing us to view difficult emotions as passing formations rather than personal failures. It opens a deep reservoir of compassion for others, seeing them not as enemies or obstacles, but as skandhas in motion. Ultimately, this analysis supports our zazen, allowing us to watch the aggregates rise and fall until we discover the boundless spaciousness underneath the dance. This flowing choreography of the aggregates is our direct, somatic entry point into śūnyatā—the radical emptiness we will explore in depth in Part 4.

The self is not a permanent thing; it is a fluid choreography. By noticing even one skandha as it arises today, we disrupt our habitual clinging. The moment we stop gripping these five passing streams, the narrow boundaries of the ego dissolve, and the vastness of the world opens up to meet us.

Dharma Talk Outline: The 12-Link Chain of Dependent Origination

1. Opening Frame (1–2 minutes)

- Start with the core statement: **"When this is, that is. When this ceases, that ceases."**
- Emphasize: This is not a theory of literal rebirth across lifetimes (though it can be read that way). It is a **moment-to-moment description of how suffering arises.**
- Nagarjuna's pivot: **If something arises dependently, it has no fixed essence. If it has no fixed essence, it can be released.**

2. The 12 Links in Order (5–6 minutes)

Present them as a *cycle of misperception* that happens in micro-moments.

1. Ignorance (Avidyā)
Not seeing things as they are; mistaking the constructed for the real.

2. Formations/Conditioning (Saṅkhāra)
Habit energies, karmic tendencies, patterned reactions.

3. Consciousness (Vijñāna)
The basic knowing that arises with each moment of experience.

4. Name-and-Form (Nāma-rūpa)
Mind and body; the structuring of experience into "me" and "world."

5. Six Sense Bases (Ṣaḍāyatana)
The senses + mind as the sixth sense.

6. Contact (Sparśa)

Sense base + object + consciousness meeting.

7. Feeling Tone (Vedanā)
Pleasant, unpleasant, or neutral.

8. Craving (Tṛṣṇā)
Grasping toward pleasant, pushing away unpleasant.

9. Clinging (Upādāna)
Fixation, identification, "This is me, this is mine."

10. Becoming (Bhava)
The momentum of identity and intention; the world solidifies.

11. Birth (Jāti)
The birth of a self-story, a role, an identity in that moment.

12. Aging-and-Death (Jarā-maraṇa)
The inevitable collapse of that constructed identity, bringing sorrow, lamentation, and suffering.
Teaching point: **This entire cycle can unfold in a single second.**

3. How to Remember the Links (1–2 minutes)
A simple mnemonic grouping:

A. The Setup (1–4)

Ignorance → Conditioning → Consciousness → Name-and-Form *This is the construction of a "self."*

B. The Interface (5–7)

Six Senses → Contact → Feeling *This is the meeting with the world.*

C. The Reaction (8–10)

Craving → Clinging → Becoming *This is where suffering gains momentum.*

D. The Result (11–12)

Birth → Aging-and-Death *This is the collapse of the identity we just built.*
Four clusters. Easy to recall under pressure.

4. The Nagarjuna Turn (2–3 minutes)
The great Buddhist philosopher clarifies the links!

A. Dependent Arising = Emptiness
Nagarjuna: **"There is nothing that is not dependently arisen. Therefore, there is nothing that is not empty."**
Meaning:
- Each link exists *only* in dependence on the previous one.
- No link has independent, permanent reality.
- Because the chain is empty, it is **not a trap** — it is **transparent**.
-

B. Emptiness = Freedom
When we see that each link is contingent:
- Craving loses its power.
- Clinging has nothing to hold onto.
- Becoming dissolves.
- Birth and death of the "self-story" stop cycling.

C. The Zen Expression
"See the chain clearly, and it breaks itself."

5. Practical Application (2–3 minutes)
Invite practitioners to notice the chain in real time:
- A sound arises (contact).
- It feels pleasant (feeling).
- You want more (craving).
- You reach for your phone (clinging).
- You become "the one who must check" (becoming).
- A whole identity is born — and collapses.

Point: **The break point is usually at feeling $\rightarrow$ craving. If we meet feeling with awareness, the rest of the chain never ignites.**

6. Closing (1 minute)

- Encourage noticing one link today — just one.
- Remind them: **"Dependent arising is not bondage; it is the doorway to freedom."**
- End with the Madhyamaka seal: **"What arises dependently is empty; what is empty is free."**

The 12-Link Chain of Dependent Origination

The core of Buddhist psychology is captured in a deceptively simple formula: *"When this is, that is. When this ceases, that ceases."* This is the foundation of Dependent Origination (*Pratītyasamutpāda*). While this twelve-link chain is traditionally studied as a literal cycle of rebirth over multiple lifetimes, we can approach it as a moment-to-moment description of how human suffering arises in micro-moments. The great master Nagarjuna offered a pivotal insight into this teaching: if something arises dependently, it has no fixed, independent essence. Because it has no fixed essence, it is empty, meaning it can be completely released.

To see how this cycle unfolds in our daily lives, we must examine the twelve links as a rapid, habitual chain reaction.

1. **Ignorance** (*Avidyā*): Not seeing reality clearly, mistaking our mental constructions for what is real.
2. **Formations** (*Saṅkhāra*): The unconscious habit energies and karmic tendencies shaped by that ignorance.
3. **Consciousness** (*Vijñāna*): The basic flash of knowing that arises with each moment of experience.
4. **Name-and-Form** (*Nāma-rūpa*): The split of raw data into a mind-and-body experience, dividing the world into "me" and "not-me."
5. **Six Sense Bases** (*Ṣaḍāyatana*): The sensory apparatus, including the mind as the sixth sense, waking up to the world.
6. **Contact** (*Sparśa*): The inevitable meeting of sense base, sense object, and consciousness.
7. **Feeling Tone** (*Vedanā*): The immediate registration of that contact as pleasant, unpleasant, or neutral.
8. **Craving** (*Tṛṣṇā*): The instinctive grasping toward the pleasant and pushing away of the unpleasant.
9. **Clinging** (*Upādāna*): Intensified craving, turning into fixation and identification: *"This is me; this is mine."*

10. **Becoming** (*Bhava*): The momentum of that identity solidifying into a distinct psychological role.
11. **Birth** (*Jāti*): The actual birth of a specific self-story, an ego-identity born to defend that role.
12. **Aging-and-Death** (*Jarā-maraṇa*): The inevitable collapse of that fragile, constructed identity, bringing sorrow, frustration, and suffering.

The Four Clusters of the Chain

To remember this twelve-link progression easily when teaching or practicing, group the links into four functional clusters:

- **The Setup (Links 1–4):** Ignorance, Conditioning, Consciousness, and Name-and-Form. This is the background construction of a separate "self."
- **The Interface (Links 5–7):** Senses, Contact, and Feeling. This is our raw, energetic meeting with the world.
- **The Reaction (Links 8–10):** Craving, Clinging, and Becoming. This is where habitual suffering gains momentum and solidifies.
- **The Result (Links 11–12):** Birth and Aging-and-Death. This is the ultimate collapse of the artificial identity we just constructed.

Nagarjuna's profound turn completely changes how we relate to this machinery. He noted that there is nothing in existence that is not dependently arisen; therefore, there is nothing that is not empty of a separate self. Because each link exists only in absolute dependence on the previous link, no single link possesses independent, permanent reality. The chain is empty, meaning it is not a solid iron trap. It is completely transparent. When we see this contingency clearly, craving loses its grip, clinging finds nothing to hold onto, becoming dissolves, and the endless birth and death of our exhausting self-stories simply cease to cycle. In Zen, we say: *"See the chain clearly, and it breaks itself."*

In our practical application, we can witness this entire sequence unfold in a single second. An email notification banner flashes across your screen—that is contact. A feeling tone of anxiety or eager anticipation instantly registers—that is feeling. You instantly crave resolution, leaning toward the screen. You click the banner, entering the grip of clinging. You are now fully embodying the persona of "the stressed worker who must reply right now"—that is becoming and birth. Within minutes, the email thread goes nowhere, leaving you drained and frustrated, which is the aging and death of that specific micro-identity.

The ultimate break point of this entire momentum sits squarely between feeling tone and craving. If we can meet raw feeling tone with clear, non-judgmental awareness on the meditation cushion or in everyday life, the match is never struck, and the rest of the chain never ignites.

We can commit to noticing just one single link in this chain today. Remember that dependent arising is not a sentence of permanent bondage to our habits; it is the wide-open doorway to our liberation. What arises dependently is empty; what is empty is radically free.

PART 3 - The Roots of Delusion & Karma

Dharma Talk Outline: Dukkha — Understanding Suffering in the Zen Path

1. Opening Frame (1–2 minutes)

Begin with the Buddha's first teaching: **"I teach only suffering and the end of suffering."**

Clarify that *dukkha* is not just "suffering" in the dramatic sense. It includes:

Dissatisfaction

Stress

Unease

The subtle feeling that "something is off"

The friction of wanting reality to be different

Teaching point: **Dukkha is not a flaw in us — it is a feature of conditioned existence.**

2. The Three Types of Dukkha (3–4 minutes)

A. Ordinary Suffering (Dukkha-dukkha)

Physical and emotional pain: illness, loss, conflict, grief. Universal, unavoidable, deeply human.

Practice pointer: **Meet pain with compassion, not resistance.**

B. Suffering of Change (Vipariṇāma-dukkha)

Pleasure fades. Situations shift. People change. Even joy is tinged with fragility.

Practice pointer: **Notice the grasping behind the fear of loss.**

C. Suffering of Conditioned Existence (Saṅkhāra-dukkha)

The most subtle form. The background hum of being a self in a world of impermanence. The tension of holding up "me" moment after moment.

Practice pointer: **See the effort of selfing — and relax it.**

3. The Zen Angle: Dukkha as a Doorway (2–3 minutes)

In Zen, suffering is not a mistake. It is the **entry point** to awakening.

Dukkha reveals where we cling.
Dukkha shows us our expectations.
Dukkha exposes our resistance to reality.
Teaching point: **Wherever you feel friction, the Dharma is already working.**

4. The Causes of Dukkha (3–4 minutes)
Tie this to the Three Poisons and Dependent Origination.

A. Craving (Greed)
Wanting things to be different.

B. Aversion (Anger)
Rejecting what is here.

C. Ignorance (Delusion)
Not seeing things as they are.
Show how these arise in micro-moments:
A sound you don't like
A thought you wish you didn't have
A feeling you want to escape
Teaching point: **Dukkha is born the moment we argue with reality.**

5. The Practice: Turning Toward Suffering (3–4 minutes)
Introduce the Zen method of meeting dukkha:

A. Mindfulness
See the suffering clearly. Name it. Feel it in the body.

B. Compassion
Hold the suffering gently. No judgment. No fixing.

C. Wisdom
Recognize impermanence. Recognize non-self. Recognize that suffering is a process, not a punishment.
Zen expression: **"When suffering is understood, it becomes compassion."**

6. Dukkha and the Path of Liberation (2–3 minutes)
Tie this to the Four Noble Truths:
There is suffering.
Suffering has causes.
Suffering can end.
There is a path.
But emphasize the Zen nuance: **We don't escape suffering —
we wake up within it.**
Dukkha becomes:
A teacher
A mirror
A compass
A call to presence

7. Practical Application (2 minutes)
Invite practitioners to reflect:
What form of dukkha showed up today?
What was the craving or aversion underneath it?
What happened when you stopped resisting?
Offer a simple practice: **"This is suffering. This is human.
This is workable."**

8. Closing (1 minute)
End with the essential reminder: **Dukkha is not the enemy. It
is the doorway to awakening.**
Encourage practitioners to meet one moment of discomfort
today with curiosity rather than resistance.

Dukkha: The Fabric of Experience and the Doorway to Awakening

The historical Buddha famously summarized his entire lifetime of teaching in a single, uncompromising declaration: *"I teach only suffering and the end of suffering."* To ears attuned to modern self-help narratives, this statement can sound remarkably bleak. Within Buddhist psychology, however, the term **dukkha** carries a far subtler, more profound meaning than dramatic physical or emotional agony alone. It encompasses everyday dissatisfaction, chronic stress, emotional unease, and that persistent background whisper telling us that something is always slightly off. It is the existential friction we experience the exact moment we want reality to be different than it actually is. *Dukkha* is never a personal flaw or a psychological failure; it is an inherent feature of conditioned existence.

To work effectively with this friction, we must recognize the three distinct layers through which it manifests in our lives.

- **Ordinary Suffering** (*Dukkha-dukkha*): The obvious physical and emotional pain that comes with being human, such as illness, injury, loss, conflict, and grief. This layer is entirely universal and unavoidable. We practice here not by trying to escape the pain, but by learning to meet it with profound compassion rather than bitter resistance.
- **The Suffering of Change** (*Vipariṇāma-dukkha*): The anxiety born from the law of impermanence. Material pleasures inevitably fade, stable situations shift, and the people we love grow old and change. Even our moments of highest joy are tinged with a quiet fragility because we know they cannot last. We practice with this layer by noticing the subtle, panicky grasping that hides just beneath our fear of loss.
- **The Suffering of Conditioned Existence** (*Saṅkhāra-dukkha*): The most elusive, subtle form of unease. It is the low background hum of maintaining a separate ego-

identity in a changing world. It is the sheer, exhausting tension of holding up the heavy monument of "me" moment after moment. Our practice pointer is to witness this continuous internal effort of "selfing"— and simply relax it.

The Anatomy of Friction

In the Zen tradition, suffering is never viewed as an administrative mistake or a spiritual detour. It is the direct entry point to our awakening, functioning as:

- **A Precision Mirror:** Exposing the hidden expectations we demand from the world.
- **A Revelatory Map:** Showing us exactly where we are still tightly clinging.
- **A Compass:** Pointing directly toward our deep-seated resistance to reality.
- **The Realization:** Wherever you experience psychological friction, the Dharma is already actively working.

The generation of this friction is tied directly to the mechanics of the Three Poisons and Dependent Origination. *Dukkha* is never created by external events; it is born the micro-second we decide to argue with reality. It arises through craving, when we desperately want a pleasant moment to be extended, and through aversion, when we aggressively reject an unpleasant experience that is already here. It thrives in ignorance, when we completely fail to see things as they are. This entire sequence plays out in ordinary micro-moments throughout our day: a sudden noise you do not like, an intrusive thought you wish you didn't have, or a heavy emotional feeling you want to run away from. The moment we try to push these things away, *dukkha* solidifies.

The Zen method of meeting this suffering requires us to turn directly toward it rather than engaging in our habitual patterns of numbing out or fleeing. First, we apply **Mindfulness** to see the suffering with absolute clarity, naming the experience and feeling its raw energy in the physical body. Second, we bring **Compassion**, holding the discomfort gently without a single drop of judgment or a frantic urge to fix it. Finally, we invoke **Wisdom**, recognizing the impermanence and non-self nature of the event. We see that this suffering is a fluid process rather than a permanent personal punishment. A classic Zen expression beautifully captures this inner alchemy: *"When suffering is understood, it becomes compassion."*

This understanding brings us back to the structural framework of the Four Noble Truths: acknowledging that suffering exists, identifying its causes, realizing its potential cessation, and walking the path of liberation. The unique nuance of Zen practice, however, is that we do not climb a ladder to escape from suffering into a sterile paradise. We wake up right within it. *Dukkha* ceases to be an enemy and transforms into our most intimate teacher, a mirror for our projections, a compass for our practice, and an urgent, daily call to total presence.

We can apply this medicine to our lives today by reflecting on our day with open curiosity, tracking what form of *dukkha* surfaced, what hidden craving or aversion fueled it, and what happened when we finally stopped fighting the moment. When discomfort inevitably arises, we can steady ourselves with a simple, grounded internal reflection: *"This is suffering. This is human. This is workable."* *Dukkha* is never the obstacle to a peaceful life; it is the wide-open doorway to your ultimate freedom.

Dharma Talk Outline: The Three Poisons — The Roots of Suffering

1. Opening Frame (1–2 minutes)
Introduce the Three Poisons as the root causes of all suffering in Buddhist psychology. Emphasize: "Every unwholesome state of mind can be traced back to one of these three." They are not moral failings — they are habits of perception.
Connect to practice: "When we recognize the poison in real time, the antidote appears naturally."

2. The Three Poisons (6–8 minutes total)
Present each poison as a psychological pattern, a felt experience, and a doorway to awakening.

A. Greed (Rāga) — Grasping, Wanting, Pulling Toward
Mythic Image
The hungry ghost — always reaching, never satisfied.
Psychological Form
Craving
Addiction
Consumerism
FOMO
The belief: *"If I get this, I'll be okay."*
How It Feels
Tight, forward-leaning, restless.
Practice Pointer
Notice the leaning. Ask: "What am I hoping this will fix?" The antidote: generosity and contentment.

B. Anger (Dveṣa) — Aversion, Pushing Away
Mythic Image
The hell realm — fire, conflict, rigidity.
Psychological Form
Irritation
Judgment
Self-criticism
Outrage culture

The belief: *"If this goes away, I'll be okay."*
How It Feels
Hot, contracted, armored.
Practice Pointer
Feel the contraction before the story. Ask: "Can I soften by 5%?" The antidote: loving-kindness and patience.

C. Ignorance (Avidyā) — Delusion, Not Seeing Clearly

Mythic Image
The animal realm — confusion, instinct, sleepwalking.
Psychological Form
Autopilot
Numbness
Avoidance
Spiritual bypassing
The belief: *"Nothing is wrong; I don't need to look."*
How It Feels
Foggy, dull, disconnected.
Practice Pointer
Bring curiosity to the moment. One mindful breath breaks the spell. The antidote: wisdom and clear seeing.

3. How the Poisons Feed Each Other (2 minutes)
They rarely appear alone.
Greed leads to anger when we don't get what we want.
Anger leads to ignorance when we shut down.
Ignorance leads to greed as we seek distraction.
Teaching point: "The poisons are a system — but so are the antidotes."

4. The Buddha's Medicine Cabinet (2–3 minutes)
Each poison has a natural counterforce:
Greed → Generosity
Anger → Compassion
Ignorance → Wisdom
These are not imposed from outside — they arise when we stop feeding the poison.
Zen angle: "When the grasping hand opens, generosity is already there."

5. Practical Application (2–3 minutes)

Invite practitioners to notice:
What poison showed up today?
What did it feel like in the body?
What story did the mind tell?
What antidote naturally appeared when awareness returned?
Offer a simple practice: Name it, feel it, soften it.

6. Closing (1 minute)

End with the core reminder: "The poisons are not enemies —
they are teachers. Each one points directly to the path of
freedom."
Invite practitioners to notice one moment today when a poison
arises, and meet it with curiosity rather than judgment.

The Three Poisons: The Roots of Suffering

In the rich landscape of Buddhist psychology, human suffering is not viewed as a theological sin or an irredeemable moral failing. Instead, our chronic discontent is traced back to three specific habits of perception known as the Three Poisons: greed, anger, and ignorance. Every unwholesome state of mind, every flash of anxiety, and every destructive behavioral pattern can be traced directly back to one of these three root causes. They are deeply ingrained psychological survival mechanisms that warp our view of reality. The beauty of this framework, however, is that it functions as a diagnostic map rather than a condemnation. The moment we learn to recognize a poison in real-time, its natural antidote appears right alongside it.

The first manifestation of this conditioning is **Greed** (*Rāga*), which operates as the psychological pattern of grasping, wanting, and pulling things toward us. In classical Buddhist iconography, this state is personified as a hungry ghost—a tragic being with a massive, bloated stomach but a neck as thin as a needle, leaving it perpetually reaching and never satisfied. In our modern lives, greed takes the form of consumerism, addictive behaviors, the fear of missing out, and a constant, restless search for the next hit of dopamine. Underneath all these behaviors sits a foundational, deceptive belief: *"If I can just get this one thing, I will finally be okay."* Physically, greed feels tight and forward-leaning, as if we are always tilting toward the next moment. We practice with this poison by noticing that forward-leaning energy, pausing to ask: *"What am I hoping this object or experience will fix?"* As our awareness returns, the natural antidotes of generosity and inner contentment arise to take its place.

Directly opposing greed is the second poison, **Anger** (*Dveṣa*), which manifests as aversion, rejection, and a desperate pushing away of reality. This state is illustrated by the mythic images of the hell realms, filled with blazing fires, ceaseless conflict, and rigid armor. Psychologically, we swim in this poison whenever we succumb to chronic irritation, harsh judgment, self-criticism, or the addictive rush of outrage culture. The underlying belief here is the mirror image of greed: *"If I can just make this thing go away, I will finally be okay."* Anger registers in the human body as a hot, contracted, and armored sensation, narrowing our field of vision. Our practice pointer is to feel that physical contraction before the mind can spin a complex story justifying its fury. We drop into the body and gently ask: *"Can I soften my resistance by just five percent?"* This small opening allows the antidotes of loving-kindness and patience to cool the flames.

The Interlocking Cycle

The Three Poisons rarely operate in isolation. Instead, they form a highly efficient, self-reinforcing psychological ecosystem:

- **Greed transforms into Anger** the exact moment an obstacle blocks us from getting what we desperately want.
- **Anger thickens into Ignorance** when the heat of our rage causes us to shut down, go numb, and refuse to see clearly.
- **Ignorance breeds further Greed** as the uncomfortable fog of confusion drives us to seek comfort in immediate sensory distraction.

The foundation holding this entire wheel of suffering together is the third poison, **Ignorance** (*Avidyā*). Ignorance is the state of delusion, fog, and fundamentally not seeing reality clearly. It is represented by the animal realm, a state driven by raw instinct, confusion, and psychological sleepwalking. In daily life, ignorance expresses itself as living on autopilot, emotional numbness, active avoidance of truth, and sophisticated forms of spiritual bypassing. Its comforting, dangerous belief whispers: *"Nothing is wrong; I don't need to look any deeper."* It feels heavy, dull, and profoundly disconnected. We break the spell of this fog by bringing radical curiosity to the present moment, trusting that a single, fully conscious breath can pierce through a lifetime of delusion, revealing the antidotes of wisdom and clear seeing.

The Buddha's medicine cabinet is entirely self-contained. Generosity dissolves greed, compassion melts anger, and wisdom illuminates ignorance. These antidotes are never rigid moral imperatives imposed upon us from the outside; they are the natural qualities of our own awakened mind that surface automatically whenever we stop feeding the poisons. A classic Zen expression captures this effortless transition perfectly: *"When the grasping hand opens, generosity is already right there."*

In our daily practice, we can apply this medicine through a simple three-step sequence: name it, feel it, and soften it. When a difficult moment arises, we identify the specific poison at play, observe exactly how it feels in the physical body, and allow our awareness to soften the contraction.

We can look back on our day with curiosity rather than judgment, tracking which poisons showed up, what stories the mind constructed around them, and what happened when awareness returned. The Three Poisons are never enemies to be brutally destroyed; they are our most intimate teachers. Every single time a poison arises, it points directly to the exact location of our freedom.

Dharma Talk Outline: Karma — The Most Misunderstood Teaching in America

1. Opening Frame (1–2 minutes)
- Start by naming the discomfort: *"Karma is the teaching Americans misunderstand the most — usually as punishment, fate, or cosmic justice."*
- Reframe immediately: **Karma means action. Karma means habit. Karma means momentum.**
- And the liberating point: **Karma is not what happens to you. Karma is how you respond.**

2. What Karma *Is Not* (1–2 minutes)
This is where you win the room.

A. Not punishment
There is no cosmic judge, no moral scoreboard.

B. Not fate or predestination
Karma is not "you deserve this."

C. Not a system of reward
Good deeds don't earn cosmic brownie points.

D. Not victim-blaming
Suffering is not a sign of "bad karma."
Teaching point: **Karma is not about blame — it's about understanding cause and effect.**

3. What Karma *Is* (3–4 minutes)

A. Karma = Action
Every thought, word, and deed plants a seed.

B. Karma = Habit Energy (Saṅkhāra)
We repeat patterns because they feel familiar, not because they're "destined."

C. Karma = Momentum

Actions create tendencies; tendencies create character; character shapes experience.

D. Karma = Choice

At every moment, we can interrupt the pattern.
Teaching point: **Karma is not the past controlling the present — it's the present shaping the future.**

4. The Three Types of Karma (2–3 minutes)

1. Body Karma

What we physically do.

2. Speech Karma

What we say — including tone, intention, and silence.

3. Mind Karma

Thoughts, attitudes, assumptions, and emotional habits.
Modern example:

- Body: reaching for the phone
- Speech: snapping at someone
- Mind: "I'm overwhelmed" These reinforce each other. That's karma.

5. The Zen Twist: Karma Is Empty (2–3 minutes)

Here's where you bring in the Madhyamaka flavor again.

A. Karma is dependently arisen

It exists only through causes and conditions.

B. What is dependently arisen is empty

No action has a fixed, permanent essence.

C. What is empty is transformable

If karma were solid, we'd be stuck forever. Because it's empty, **freedom is always possible.**

D. Zen expression

"Karma is not a prison — it's a classroom."

6. Breaking Karma in Real Time (2–3 minutes)

A. Awareness interrupts momentum
The moment we see a habit clearly, it loses power.

B. Small shifts matter
One mindful breath changes the trajectory of the next moment.

C. The "gap"
Between stimulus and response, there is a space. In that space, karma dissolves.

D. Practical example
- Someone criticizes you.
- Old karma: defensiveness, anger, withdrawal.
- New karma: pause, breathe, respond with clarity.

Teaching point: **Karma is not what happens — karma is what you do next.**

7. Closing (1 minute)
- Invite practitioners to notice one karmic habit today — just one.
- Encourage them to meet it with curiosity, not shame.
- End with a line that lands well in modern ears: **"Karma is not destiny. Karma is practice."**

Karma: The Most Misunderstood Teaching

Karma is perhaps the teaching that is misunderstood most frequently, appearing in popular culture as a system of cosmic punishment, fate, or moral justice. We hear it invoked when bad things happen to bad people, or when someone experiences an unexpected stroke of luck. This view turns a profound psychological teaching into a giant scoreboard in the sky, however, which misses the point entirely. In the Buddhist tradition, karma means action, habit, and momentum. The most liberating aspect of this teaching is simple: karma is not what happens to you; karma is how you choose to respond.

To understand this clearly, we must first dismantle what karma is not.

- It is **not punishment**, because there is no cosmic judge handing out sentences.
- It is **not fate** or predestination; the Dharma completely rejects the idea that your life is pre-written.
- It is **not a reward system** where good deeds earn spiritual brownie points to be cashed in later.
- Most importantly, it is **not a tool for victim-blaming**.

When someone experiences tragedy or structural oppression, it is a cruel distortion of the Dharma to claim their suffering is the result of "bad karma." Karma is never about tracking blame; it is about understanding the natural law of cause and effect.

True karma operates as a living psychological process. Every single thought, word, and deed plants a seed in the fertile ground of our consciousness. These seeds develop into habit energy (*saṅkhāra*). We repeat painful patterns in our relationships and behaviors not because we are destined to do so, but simply because those patterns feel familiar to the ego. This repetition creates a powerful momentum. Our individual actions create tendencies, these tendencies harden into character, and our character ultimately shapes how we experience reality. Karma is never the past controlling the present moment; it is the choices we make in the present shaping our future.

We generate this momentum through three distinct avenues: body karma, speech karma, and mind karma.

1. **Body Karma** consists of our physical movements and gestures, such as aggressively slamming a door or reaching automatically for a smartphone.
2. **Speech Karma** includes the words we choose, our underlying tone of voice, and even our intentional silences.
3. **Mind Karma** involves our hidden thoughts, knee-jerk assumptions, and deep emotional habits.

Consider a common modern sequence: an anxious thought arises in the mind (*mind karma*), causing us to snap irritably at a family member (*speech karma*), which leads us to physically storm out of the room (*body karma*). These three expressions reinforce each other in a closed loop. That loop is the very definition of karma.

The Classroom of the Mind

By looking through the lens of Madhyamaka philosophy, we discover the Zen twist to this teaching:

- **Karma is dependently arisen:** It exists solely through changing causes and conditions.
- **Karma is empty:** No habit or past action possesses a fixed, permanent, unalterable essence.
- **Karma is transformable:** Because it is empty of a solid core, it can be shifted, reshaped, and dissolved completely.
- **The Realization:** Karma is not a prison house; it is a classroom for waking up.

We break the momentum of our karma in real-time by inserting awareness into our daily routines. The moment we see an old habit clearly, its automatic power begins to wither. One single mindful breath changes the trajectory of the next ten minutes, interrupting a potential spiral of reactivity. This practice is about finding the gap. Between the external stimulus and our internal response, there is a tiny fraction of a second where space opens up. In that space, karma dissolves, and true freedom is born.

If someone criticizes your work, for example, your old karma might urge you to become instantly defensive, angry, or cold. By resting in awareness, you can pause, feel the heat of the emotion in your body, and choose a completely new path. You respond with clarity rather than reacting out of conditioning. Karma is not the trigger; karma is what you decide to do next.

We can practice with this today by noticing just one karmic habit without an ounce of shame or self-judgment. Approach the habit with the open curiosity of a scientist observing an experiment. Karma is never your destiny. Karma is simply your practice.

PART 4 - The Heart of Mahāyāna & Zen

Dharma Talk Outline: Sunyata — The Heart of Mahāyāna

1. Opening Frame (1–2 minutes)
- Start with the simplest possible definition: **Sunyata = emptiness = interdependence = lack of fixed essence.**
- Emphasize: **Emptiness is not nihilism. Emptiness is not nothingness. Emptiness is freedom.**
- Quote the Heart Sutra (one line is safe and powerful): *"Form is emptiness; emptiness is form."*

2. What Emptiness *Is Not* (1–2 minutes)
This clears away the biggest misconceptions.

A. Not "nothing matters"
Emptiness is not apathy.

B. Not a metaphysical void
It's not a cosmic vacuum.

C. Not a denial of the world
Things exist — just not independently.

D. Not a belief system
It's a way of seeing.
Teaching point: **Emptiness is the absence of fixed, separate, permanent identity.**

3. What Emptiness *Is* (3–4 minutes)
This is the heart of the talk.

A. Emptiness = Dependent Arising
Nagarjuna's core insight: **"Whatever is dependently arisen is empty."** Meaning:
- Everything exists *because* of causes and conditions.
- Nothing stands alone.
- Nothing has a permanent core.

B. Emptiness = Interbeing
Thich Nhat Hanh's language: A flower contains sunshine, rain, soil, time, the gardener — nothing is "just itself."

C. Emptiness frees us from perfectionism
No fixed self means no fixed failure.
Because nothing is fixed, everything is workable. This is the liberating part.

D. Emptiness = Middle Way
Not existence, not non-existence. Not eternalism, not nihilism. A dynamic, relational reality.

4. The Three Levels of Emptiness (2–3 minutes)
This gives structure and depth.

1. Emptiness of Self
No fixed "I." The self is a process, not a thing.

2. Emptiness of Phenomena
Objects, emotions, thoughts — all arise dependently.

3. Emptiness of Emptiness
Even emptiness is empty — not a final truth to cling to. This prevents turning emptiness into a dogma.
Teaching point: **Emptiness is not a belief — it's a tool for loosening the grip of clinging.**

5. Why Emptiness Matters (2–3 minutes)
Bring it down to lived experience.

A. Emptiness dissolves suffering
Suffering comes from taking things as solid:
- "This emotion defines me."
- "This situation will never change."
- "This person is always like this."

Emptiness reveals: **Everything is fluid. Everything is workable.**

B. Emptiness opens compassion

If there is no separate self, then your suffering and mine are intertwined.

C. Emptiness frees us from perfectionism

No fixed self means no fixed failure.

D. Emptiness makes joy possible

When we stop clinging, we can finally participate in life.

6. Practicing Emptiness (2–3 minutes)

Make it practical.

A. Notice the constructed nature of experience

Thoughts arise and pass. Emotions arise and pass. Identities arise and pass.

B. Ask: "What is this dependent on?"

A powerful, simple inquiry.

C. Relax the grip

Emptiness is not something you "achieve." It's what appears when clinging relaxes.

D. Just sit

Zazen is the direct experience of emptiness — not thinking about it, but resting in it.

7. Closing (1 minute)

- Bring it home: **"Emptiness is not the destruction of the world — it is the freeing of the world."**
- Invite practitioners to notice one moment today where they can soften their grip.
- End with the Heart Sutra's essence: **"Because all things are empty, all things are possible."**

Sunyata: The Heart of Mahāyāna

The concept of *śūnyatā*—translated as emptiness—is arguably the most radical and liberating insight in the entire Mahāyāna Buddhist tradition. It is also the most frequently misunderstood. To enter this teaching safely, we must begin with its simplest possible definition: emptiness is interdependence, the total lack of any fixed, permanent, or separate essence in things. Emptiness is not a dark, pessimistic nihilism, nor is it a cold philosophy of nothingness. Emptiness is freedom. The Heart Sutra famously captures this paradox in a single line: *'Form is emptiness; emptiness is form.''* This is a direct declaration that the everyday world we see, hear, and touch is entirely inseparable from boundless, open spaciousness.

To comprehend this truth, we must clear away the misconceptions that routinely trap the intellect.

- Emptiness is **not apathy**, and it never means "nothing matters."
- It is **not a metaphysical void** or a cosmic vacuum waiting at the end of the universe.
- It is **not a denial of our world**, because things do exist; they simply do not exist independently.
- Most importantly, emptiness is **not a belief system** to adopt.

It is a direct, operational way of seeing. It points to the complete absence of any fixed, separate identity in ourselves and the world around us.

The great master Nagarjuna provided the philosophical anchor for this teaching, demonstrating that whatever is dependently arisen is empty. Nothing stands entirely alone; everything exists solely because of a web of changing causes and conditions. The late master Thich Nhat Hanh beautifully illuminated this reality through his concept of "interbeing." He noted that if you look closely at a single flower, you will see that it contains sunshine, rain, soil, minerals, time, and the care of the gardener. The flower is entirely empty of a separate self, yet it is simultaneously full of the entire cosmos. Nothing is ever "just itself." Because nothing is frozen in place, reality is perfectly fluid, dynamic, and workable. This is the Middle Way: a relational reality that avoids the twin traps of eternalism and nihilism.

The Levels of Insight

To help navigate this depth on the meditation cushion, the tradition breaks emptiness down into three distinct structural levels:

- **Emptiness of Self:** Recognizing that the ego is a shifting, fluid process rather than a permanent entity.
- **Emptiness of Phenomena:** Seeing that external objects, thoughts, and emotions arise dependently and hold no solid core.
- **Emptiness of Emptiness:** Realizing that even the concept of emptiness is empty, preventing us from turning a useful tool into a rigid dogma.

Bringing this teaching down into our lived human experience is what dissolves our psychological suffering. We suffer primarily because we mistake passing experiences for solid, unyielding monuments. We tell ourselves stories like: *"This painful emotion defines who I am," "This difficult situation will never change,"* or *"This person is permanently flawed."* Emptiness shatters these illusions by revealing that everything is a flowing stream.

This realization naturally opens the floodgates of compassion. If there is no rigid wall separating "me" from "you," then your suffering and my suffering are deeply intertwined. This insight frees us from the paralyzing grip of perfectionism; because there is no fixed self, there is no such thing as a fixed, permanent failure. When we stop desperately gripping reality, we can finally participate in the joy of life.

We practice with emptiness not by trying to achieve a mystical state, but by relaxing our habit of grasping. In our daily lives, we can look at a heavy emotion or a stressful situation and gently ask: *"What is this dependent on?"* We trace the roots of the experience to its passing causes, watching the initial solidity dissolve. Ultimately, our formal zazen is the direct, non-conceptual embodiment of this truth. We sit on the cushion, allow thoughts and identities to arise and pass without holding onto them, and rest in the vast spaciousness that remains.

Emptiness is never the destruction of our world; it is the freeing of our world. It invites us to move through our day with a lighter, softer grip on our opinions, our identities, and our expectations. Because all things are empty of a rigid script, all things are completely possible.

Dharma Talk Outline: The Heart Sutra — A Practice Manual for Emptiness and Everyday Life

1. Opening Frame (1–2 minutes)
- Introduce the Heart Sutra as the distilled essence of Mahāyāna wisdom.
- Emphasize: **"This is not a philosophical text — it's a manual for how to practice."**
- One line you *can* quote safely: *"Form is emptiness; emptiness is form."*
- The sutra is short because it's meant to be lived, not analyzed.

2. The Setting: Avalokiteśvara in Deep Samadhi (1–2 minutes)
- The sutra begins with Avalokiteśvara — the Bodhisattva of Compassion — practicing profound prajñā.
- This is important: **Compassion is the one who realizes emptiness.**
- Emptiness is not cold; it's the ground of compassion.

Practice point

When we sit, we are Avalokiteśvara — turning the light inward, seeing clearly.

3. The Five Skandhas Are Empty (2–3 minutes)
- Avalokiteśvara sees that the Five Skandhas are empty of fixed essence.
- This is the sutra's first instruction: **Look directly at your experience and see its fluidity.**

How this guides practice
- Body: sensations arise and pass.
- Feelings: pleasant/unpleasant/neutral — none solid.
- Perceptions: labels that come and go.
- Formations: thoughts/emotions as weather.
- Consciousness: a stream, not a self.

Teaching point

The Heart Sutra is telling us how to sit: watch the Skandhas without clinging.

4. "No Eye, No Ear, No Nose…" — The Deconstruction of Experience (2–3 minutes)
- This long list is not nihilism — it's a training.
- The sutra is dismantling the machinery of reactivity.

Meaning
- "No eye" = don't cling to the sense organ.
- "No form" = don't cling to the object.
- "No eye-consciousness" = don't cling to the experience.

Practice point
Let experience arise without building a self around it. This is zazen in a nutshell.

5. "No Suffering, No Cause, No Cessation, No Path" (2 minutes)
- This is not a denial of the Four Noble Truths.
- It's the *emptiness* of the Four Noble Truths.

Meaning
- Even the teachings are empty — don't cling to them.
- The path is a raft, not a doctrine.

Practice point
Use the teachings, but don't turn them into identity or ideology.

6. "No Attainment and Nothing to Attain" (1–2 minutes)
- This is the heart of Zen.

Meaning
- Awakening is not an achievement.
- There is no "enlightened self" waiting at the end of the path.

Practice point
Sit without gaining idea. Practice without chasing a result. Awakening appears when grasping relaxes.

7. The Mantra — Gate Gate Pāragate Pārasaṃgate Bodhi Svāhā (2 minutes)

- You don't need to quote it fully — just reference it.
- This is the only mantra in the sutra, and it's a summary of the whole teaching.

Meaning
- *Gate* — gone
- *Gate* — gone
- *Pāragate* — gone beyond
- *Pārasaṃgate* — gone completely beyond
- *Bodhi Svāhā* — awakening, hallelujah

Practice point
Let go, let go, let go beyond letting go. This is the rhythm of practice.

8. The Heart Sutra as a Practice Manual (2–3 minutes)
Tie it all together:

A. Sit like Avalokiteśvara
Compassionate, steady, open.

B. Watch the Skandhas
See their emptiness in real time.

C. Don't cling to sense experience
Let the world flow through you.

D. Don't cling to teachings
Use them lightly.

E. Don't chase attainment
Practice with nothing to gain.

F. Let go, again and again
This is the mantra of the path.

9. Closing (1 minute)
- Bring it home: **"The Heart Sutra is not telling us what reality is — it's telling us how to meet reality."**

- Invite practitioners to let one moment today be "form is emptiness, emptiness is form."
- End with: **"When we stop clinging, the heart becomes vast."**

The Heart Sutra: A Practice Manual for Emptiness and Everyday Life

The Heart Sutra is often approached as the towering peak of Mahāyāna Buddhist philosophy—a dense, paradoxical text to be picked apart by scholars. If we treat it merely as an intellectual puzzle, however, we miss its true pulse. The Heart Sutra is not a philosophical treatise; it is a manual for how to practice. Its brevity is intentional. It was not written to be analyzed from a distance, but to be lived, breathed, and embodied in the laboratory of our daily lives. At its core, the sutra's most famous declaration, "Form is emptiness; emptiness is form," is not an abstract metaphysical formula. It is a direct description of what happens when we sit down on the cushion and open our eyes to the world.

To understand how to use this manual, we must look at how it begins: with Avalokiteśvara, the Bodhisattva of Compassion, resting in deep samadhi. This setting carries profound operational weight. It tells us that wisdom and compassion are entirely inseparable. Emptiness is not a cold, nihilistic void, nor is it a detached psychological state. Emptiness is the very ground of compassion. Because nothing has a fixed, separate self, we are completely interconnected with all things. When we sit in meditation, we are acting as Avalokiteśvara. We turn our light inward, looking clearly at our experience, realizing that true compassion arises only when the rigid walls of the ego begin to soften.

From this state of deep stillness, the sutra delivers its first practical instruction: look directly at the five *skandhas*—the components that make up our entire human experience—and see their fluidity. The sutra is instructing us precisely how to sit in zazen.

- We observe the **body** and see that physical sensations arise and pass.

- We notice **feelings**—pleasant, unpleasant, and neutral—and realize none of them are solid.
- Our **perceptions** and labels come and go; our mental **formations**, the thoughts and emotions that feel so overwhelming, are revealed to be nothing more than passing weather.
- Even **consciousness** itself is a flowing stream, not a permanent self.

By watching the *skandhas* without clinging, we learn to witness our life in real-time without freezing it into a rigid identity.

As the text unfolds, it enters a famous, sweeping deconstruction of our sensory world: *"No eye, no ear, no nose..."* This long list of negations is not a denial of reality, but a systematic dismantling of the machinery of human reactivity. It is a training manual for letting go. When the sutra says "no eye," it means do not cling to the sense organ. "No form" means do not cling to the object of sight. "No eye-consciousness" means do not cling to the experience of seeing. In the midst of zazen, this is our practice: we allow sights, sounds, and smells to arise naturally, without building a frantic, defensive "self" around them. We let the world move through us without grabbing onto it.

The sutra then takes a radical turn, deconstructing Buddhism itself: *"No suffering, no cause, no cessation, no path."* This is the emptiness of the Four Noble Truths. It serves as a stark warning for practitioners not to turn the teachings into a rigid ideology or a new badge of identity. The Dharma is a raft to cross the river, not a monument to carry on our backs. We use the teachings lightly, skillfully, and with humility, remembering that even the path itself must eventually be let go.

This leads to the absolute heart of Zen practice: *"No attainment and nothing to attain."* In our ordinary lives, we are driven by a gaining mind; we practice to get smarter, calmer, or more spiritual. Awakening is not an achievement, however, and there is no "enlightened self" waiting for us at the finish line. True practice means sitting without a gaining idea, abandoning the urge to chase a spiritual result. Awakening appears naturally the exact moment our grasping relaxes.

The entire journey of the sutra is ultimately distilled into a single, vibrant mantra: *Gate gate pāragate pārasaṃgate bodhi svāhā.* Gone, gone, gone beyond, gone completely beyond—awakening, hallelujah! This is the rhythmic pulse of the meditative life: let go, let go, and then let go of letting go.

The Practice Framework

To bring the Heart Sutra off the page and into your life, remember these six core movements:

- **Sit like Avalokiteśvara:** Be compassionate, steady, and utterly open to what is.
- **Watch the skandhas:** Witness the fluid, changing nature of your thoughts and sensations in real-time.
- **Don't cling to sense experience:** Let the world flow through you without friction.
- **Don't cling to the teachings:** Use the Dharma as a tool, never as an ideology.
- **Don't chase attainment:** Practice with nothing to gain, leaving no room for the ego.
- **Let go, again and again:** Embody the rhythm of the mantra in every breath.

Ultimately, the Heart Sutra is not trying to tell us *what* reality is; it is showing us *how to meet* reality. It invites us to step out of our concepts and inhabit our lives directly. Today, let just one single moment be an expression of this truth: look at a passing emotion or a physical sensation and see that "form is emptiness, emptiness is form." When we finally stop clinging to our small stories, the heart naturally opens, revealing a vast and boundless freedom.

Dharma Talk Outline: Don't-Know Mind — Only Go Straight

1. Opening Frame (1–2 minutes)

Begin with Seung Sahn's essential teaching: **"Only don't know."**

Clarify that don't-know mind is not ignorance, confusion, or passivity. It is **the mind before thinking** — clear, open, responsive, alive.

Teaching point: **Don't-know mind is the foundation of Zen practice and the expression of awakening.**

2. What Don't-Know Mind Is (3–4 minutes)

A. The Mind Before Thinking
The moment before a thought appears. The space in which all thoughts arise and dissolve.

B. Pure Awareness
Not blankness. Not dullness. A vivid, direct presence.

C. The Zen Angle
Don't-know mind is the same as:
Beginner's mind
Emptiness
Suchness
Original nature
Buddha-mind
Different words, same reality.
D. Practice Pointer

"Put it all down." Let go of opinions, stories, judgments — even for one breath.

3. Why Don't-Know Mind Matters (3–4 minutes)

A. Thinking Cannot Solve Suffering

The thinking mind creates duality, comparison, and conflict.

B. Don't-Know Cuts Through Delusion

When we drop thinking, we drop the self that clings to thinking.

C. Don't-Know Opens Compassion

Without fixed views, the heart becomes flexible and responsive.

D. Don't-Know Reveals Wisdom

Wisdom is not knowledge — it is clarity without concepts.
Teaching point: Don't-know mind is the doorway to freedom.

4. "Only Go Straight" — The Path of Directness (2–3 minutes)

Introduce Seung Sahn's second essential phrase: "Only go straight — don't know."
Meaning:
Stay with the moment.
Stay with the question.
Stay with the practice.
Don't wander into past or future.
This is the Bodhisattva's perseverance — unwavering, wholehearted, sincere.
Practice pointer: "Just now, what is this?"

5. Don't-Know Mind and Koan Practice (3–4 minutes)

Tie this chapter to the previous one.

A. Koans Cannot Be Solved by Thinking

The moment you think, you miss it.

B. Don't-Know Is the Correct Koan Posture

Hold the hwadu lightly but constantly. Let it burn away concepts.

C. Awakening Through Don't-Know

Insight arises when the thinking mind collapses. The answer appears when the question disappears.

Teaching point: **Koans don't give you answers — they give you** don't-know.

6. Don't-Know Mind in Daily Life (3–4 minutes)

A. In Relationships
Drop your story about the other person. Meet them fresh.

B. In Conflict
Let go of being right. Listen deeply.

C. In Uncertainty
Instead of grasping for control, return to don't-know.

D. In Practice
Don't chase experiences. Don't cling to insights. Just practice.
Zen expression: "Clear mind, clear action."

7. The Paradox: Don't-Know Is Both the Path and the Fruit (2–3 minutes)
Don't-know mind is:
The beginning of practice
The method of practice
The expression of awakening
The nature of reality
You start with don't-know. You return to don't-know. You end in don't-know.
Teaching point: The more deeply you practice, the more deeply you don't know.

8. Practical Application (2 minutes)
Invite practitioners to reflect:
Where am I holding fixed views?
Where am I clinging to certainty?
Where can I soften into don't-know?
Offer a simple practice: Pause. Exhale. Ask: "What is this?" Don't answer.

9. Closing (1 minute)
End with Seung Sahn's essential teaching: "Only don't know."

And the final reminder: Don't-know mind is not the absence of wisdom — it is the birthplace of wisdom.

Don't-Know Mind: Only Go Straight

The legendary Korean Zen Master Seung Sahn once encountered a student who questioned the specific cultural forms, rituals, and lineages used in his school. The student asked why it was necessary to teach Asian-style Mahāyāna Buddhism or a particular Zen style if everything is ultimately One. Zen Master Seung Sahn's response, recorded beautifully in *The Compass of Zen*, cuts straight to the quick of all spiritual training:

"I don't teach Korean or Mahayana or Zen. I don't even teach Buddhism. I only teach don't know. Fifty years here and there teaching only don't know. So only don't know. OK?"

This is the ultimate, uncompromising core of the Zen path. Don't-know mind is not a state of uneducated ignorance, flat confusion, or passive laziness. It is the mind as it exists right before the very first movement of conceptual thought—completely clear, vast, open, instantly responsive, and vibrantly alive. It is both the immovable foundation of our formal meditation practice and the direct, unadorned expression of our true nature.

To practice effectively with this orientation, we must intimately experience what don't-know mind actually feels like. It is the literal mind before thinking occurs, representing the silent, luminous space from which all individual thoughts arise and into which they naturally dissolve. This is pure, unadulterated awareness. It contains no dullness, no blankness, and no intellectual fog; it is a vivid, direct, and spacious presence. Within the broader Buddhist tradition, we use many different names for this identical experience, calling it beginner's mind, emptiness, suchness, our original nature, or the Buddha-mind. These are merely different conventional pointers for the exact same reality. We touch this space through a simple, direct practice pointer: *"Put it all down."* We let go of our heavy opinions, our tightly held stories, and our hardwired judgments, if only for the duration of a single inhalation.

This radical dropping of our knowledge is vital because our analytical thinking mind can never solve our fundamental existential suffering. The conceptual brain is an engine of division, continuously generating dualities, comparisons, rigid preferences, and internal conflicts. The moment we drop our thinking, however, we drop the fictitious, fragile "self" that clings so desperately to those thoughts. Don't-know mind effortlessly cuts through the thick vines of our delusion. When we abandon our fixed views, the heart-mind instantly becomes flexible, spacious, and naturally compassionate, responding to the world out of clarity rather than conditioning. Wisdom is never about accumulating more spiritual information; it is simply clarity completely unburdened by concepts.

The Two Phrases of a Bodhisattva

Zen Master Seung Sahn unified this profound orientation with a second, deeply practical phrase to guide our daily lives:

- **"Only Keep Don't-Know Mind"** stabilizes our internal compass, anchoring us in the unconditioned space before thought.
- **"Only Go Straight"** drives our external practice, urging us to step forward with unwavering, wholehearted directness.
- **The Alignment:** Together, they mean staying completely with the immediate question, the immediate breath, and the immediate moment without wandering into past memories or future anxieties.

This posture provides the essential framework for working with koans, as explored in our previous chapter. A koan or a *hwadu* can never be untangled by the analytical intellect; the micro-second you try to think your way to an answer, you have completely missed the target. Don't-know is the only correct posture for this study. We learn to hold a core question like *"What am I?"* lightly but constantly, allowing its intense uncertainty to burn away our conceptual certainties. True insight flashes forward only when our logical thinking collapses under its own weight. The final answer appears only when the frantic questioner disappears into the scenery. Koans never give you intellectual answers; they give you a deep, stable don't-know.

Bringing this unconditioned mind off the cushion and into our daily lives completely revolutionizes our human relationships. When interacting with family, friends, or coworkers, we practice dropping our dusty, accumulated historical stories about who they are, choosing instead to meet them entirely fresh in the present moment. In times of interpersonal conflict, we actively let go of our exhausting obsession with being right, choosing instead to listen deeply from a space of open attention. When navigating seasons of intense external uncertainty, instead of frantically grasping for control over things we cannot predict, we learn to relax backward into don't-know. We stop chasing exotic spiritual experiences and stop clinging to our passing meditative insights. We simply practice, embodying the classic Zen expression: *"Clear mind, clear action."*

This training presents us with a beautiful spiritual paradox: don't-know mind is simultaneously the path and the fruit of realization. It is the very beginning of our practice, the method of our practice, the expression of our awakening, and the ultimate nature of reality itself. You start your journey in don't-know, you return to don't-know throughout the trials of life, and you end your journey right back in don't-know. The deeper your practice matures, the more profoundly you realize you do not know a single thing.

We can apply this medicine to our lives today by looking honestly at where we are currently holding rigid, fixed views, where we are desperately clinging to artificial certainty, and where we can afford to soften into space. We can pause right now, exhale fully, and ask our entire body: *"What is this?"* Do not let the mind manufacture an answer. Don't-know mind is never the absence of wisdom. It is the wide-open, infinite birthplace of all true wisdom, waiting for you right here in this very breath.

Dharma Talk Outline: Koans — How to Study and How to Awaken

1. Opening Frame (1–2 minutes)

Begin by reframing koans for modern practitioners:
Koans are not riddles.
They are not puzzles to solve.
They are mirrors that reveal the nature of mind.
Introduce the core teaching: "A koan is not about the past; it is about your mind *right now*."
Briefly acknowledge the two major approaches:
American Zen: study dozens or hundreds of koans in sequence.
Korean Seon: work deeply with one or two *hwadu* for a lifetime.
Teaching point: Both aim at the same thing — direct awakening.

2. What a Koan Actually Is (2–3 minutes)

A. A Koan Is a Pointing-Out Instruction

It points directly to:
Don't-know mind
Non-duality
The collapse of conceptual thinking
The immediacy of this moment

B. A Koan Is a Mirror

It reflects:
Your habits
Your assumptions
Your identity
Your clarity or confusion

C. A Koan Is a Catalyst

It is designed to frustrate the thinking mind until something deeper opens.

3. The Two Major Approaches (3–4 minutes)

A. The American / Japanese Approach: Many Koans

Students work through a curriculum of 100–300 koans.
Each koan tests a different facet of insight.
The emphasis is on breadth, variety, and demonstration of understanding.
Strength: A wide range of perspectives and challenges.
Risk: Insight becomes performative or intellectual.

B. The Korean Seon Approach: One Hwadu

A practitioner may work with one hwadu for years or decades.
The hwadu is the "head word," the living spark of the koan.
The goal is not solving but becoming completely absorbed.
Examples:
"What is this?"
"What am I?"
"What is the sound of one hand?"
"What is Buddha?"
Strength: Depth, stability, and unshakable clarity.
Risk: Impatience or discouragement if progress is misunderstood.
Teaching point: Many koans or one koan — the real question is: Are you practicing with your whole life?

4. Zen Master Seung Sahn's Method: Situation, Function, Relationship (4–5 minutes)

Introduce this as a uniquely clear and practical way to evaluate a koan.

A. Situation

What is happening in the story? Not the meaning — the *situation*.
Who is speaking? What is the context? What is the energy?

Example: A monk asks, "Does a dog have Buddha-nature?"
Situation: A sincere question meets a sharp teaching moment.

B. Function

How does the teaching function in that moment? What is the teacher *doing*? Cutting? Encouraging? Redirecting? Shattering concepts?
Example: Joshu answers "Mu!" Function: Cutting off conceptual thinking.

C. Relationship

How does this apply to your life right now? Not in theory — in this moment, this breath, this situation.
Example: When someone asks you a sincere question, how do you respond? With clarity? With presence? With don't-know mind?
Teaching point: A koan is alive only when it becomes your life.

5. How to Work with a Koan (3–4 minutes)

A. Don't Try to Solve It

Koans are not intellectual. The more you think, the further you get.

B. Hold the Hwadu Lightly but Constantly

Let it permeate your walking, sitting, eating, breathing.

C. Let Frustration Ripen

When the thinking mind exhausts itself, insight appears.

D. Trust Don't-Know Mind

This is the heart of Seung Sahn's teaching.
Don't-know mind is:
Clear

Open
Responsive
Alive

E. Awakening Is Not an Answer

It is a shift in perception. A dropping away. A moment of intimacy with reality.

6. The Moment of Awakening (2–3 minutes)

Describe awakening not as fireworks but as:
A sudden clarity
A collapse of duality
A direct seeing
A return to simplicity
Teaching point: Awakening is not the end of koan practice — it is the beginning of living it.

7. Practical Application (2 minutes)

Invite practitioners to reflect:
What is your hwadu right now?
What question is alive in your life?
Where is your don't-know mind?
Offer a simple practice: "What is this?" Ask it with your whole body.

8. Closing (1 minute)

End with Seung Sahn's essential teaching: **"Only don't know."**

And the reminder: **A koan is not a story from the past — it is the doorway to your own awakening, right now.**

Koans: How to Study and How to Awaken

Koans are frequently romanticized in Western culture as exotic, paradoxical riddles or intellectual puzzles designed to trick the mind. In our practice, however, we reframe them completely: koans are not riddles, they are not puzzles to solve, and they are not intellectual games. They are precision mirrors that reveal the true nature of the mind. A koan is never about a historical event in the past; it is a direct reflection of your mind right now in this very second. Within the global Zen community, two major structural approaches to this study have emerged. The American and Japanese traditions typically guide students through a structured curriculum of dozens or hundreds of koans in sequence, testing different facets of insight. Conversely, the traditional Korean Seon approach emphasizes working deeply with just one or two *hwadu*—the living spark or "head word" of a koan—for an entire lifetime. Both methodologies look at the exact same moon, aiming directly at immediate, unconditioned awakening.

To practice effectively with these dynamic teaching tools, we must understand what a koan actually does. It functions as a direct pointing-out instruction, steering us away from conceptual descriptions and launching us straight into "don't-know mind," non-duality, and the absolute immediacy of the present moment. Because it acts as a mirror, a koan mercilessly reflects your personal habits, your hidden assumptions, your rigid identities, and your current state of clarity or confusion. It serves as a psychological catalyst, deliberately frustrating the logical, analytical mind until our habitual thinking structures exhaust themselves and something infinitely deeper breaks open.

We can see this clearly by contrasting the two primary training models. In the American and Japanese approach, a student navigates a vast matrix of one hundred to three hundred individual cases. Each case challenges a specific nuance of understanding, emphasizing a breadth of perspective. The strength of this method lies in its versatility, though it carries a distinct risk of turning insight into something intellectual or performative. The traditional Korean Seon approach focuses entirely on depth and stability. A practitioner might sit with a single *hwadu*—such as *"What is this?"*, *"What am I?"*, or Chao-chou's famous *"Mu"*—for years or even decades. The objective here is not to find a clever answer, but to become completely absorbed by the question until the boundary between the questioner and the question dissolves entirely. Whether you work with many koans or a single *hwadu*, the operational question remains identical: are you practicing with your whole life?

The Framework of Master Seung Sahn

To bring an analytical clarity to this profound practice, the great Korean Zen Master Seung Sahn organized koan study into three distinct, highly practical investigative dimensions:

- **Situation:** Discerning exactly what is happening on the raw surface of the story, identifying the specific context, the characters, and the energetic tone without adding commentary.
- **Function:** Examining how the teaching operates in that precise moment, observing exactly what the teacher is doing to cut, redirect, or shatter the student's conceptual trap.
- **Relationship:** Translating the case directly into your immediate life, testing how its living truth manifests in your current breath, your current relationships, and your current actions.

Applying this methodology requires a radical shift in how we utilize our intelligence. First and foremost, you must completely abandon the urge to solve the koan intellectually, because the more you think, the further you wander from the target. We learn to hold the *hwadu* lightly but continuously, allowing the question to permeate our walking, our sitting, our eating, and our working. When the inevitable frustration arises, we do not run away; we allow that frustration to ripen, knowing that insight blossoms only when the thinking mind hits a dead end.

This process relies entirely on trusting "don't-know mind." In Master Seung Sahn's teaching, don't-know mind is not a state of ignorant blankness. It is our natural, original mind—completely clear, vast, open, instantly responsive, and vibrantly alive. Awakening within this lineage is never experienced as a dramatic fireworks display or the acquisition of a secret piece of knowledge. It is a sudden, quiet return to simplicity, a complete collapse of the artificial duality between self and world, and a moment of total intimacy with reality exactly as it is. It is not the final end of our practice, but the true beginning of living it.

We can activate this investigative energy right now by identifying the core question that is genuinely alive in our own lives today. We can step directly into our don't-know mind by asking ourselves with our entire physical body: *"What is this?"* Master Seung Sahn distilled the essence of all spiritual training into three simple words: *"Only don't know."* A koan is never a dusty museum piece from ancient Asia; it is the wide-open doorway to your own immediate awakening, waiting for you right here in this very breath.

PART 5 - The Bodhisattva Vow in Action

Dharma Talk Outline: The Influence of the Feminine in the Life of the Buddha

1. Opening Frame (1–2 minutes)
- Begin with a reframing: *"The Buddha did not awaken in isolation. His life was shaped, supported, and challenged by women at every stage."*
- Emphasize that in Buddhism, "feminine" does not mean gender alone — it also refers to qualities: **nurturing, intuition, relational wisdom, compassion, embodiment, and fierce clarity.**
- This talk highlights the women — and the feminine principles — that shaped the Buddha's path.

2. Queen Māyā — The First Teacher (1–2 minutes)

A. Birth through the Feminine
- Queen Māyā dreams of a white elephant entering her side — a symbol of sacred conception.
- She gives birth standing, holding a tree branch — grounded, embodied, powerful.
- She dies seven days later, but her presence sets the tone: **Awakening begins in the body, through a woman's courage and sacrifice.**

B. Symbolic Teaching
- Māyā represents **the mystery of emergence**, the creative force of life.
- Her death reminds us: **Even the Buddha's life begins with loss — a profoundly human experience.**

3. Mahāpajāpatī Gotamī — The First Feminist in the Sangha (2–3 minutes)
A. The Buddha's Aunt and Stepmother
- She raises Siddhartha after Māyā's death — the Buddha's first experience of maternal compassion.
- After his awakening, she becomes the first woman to request ordination.

B. Her Persistence

- The Buddha initially refuses.
- She and 500 women walk barefoot for miles, shaving their heads, wearing robes, standing at the gates of Vesāli.

C. The Turning Point

- Ānanda advocates on their behalf.
- The Buddha relents — not out of concession, but recognition: **Women are fully capable of awakening.**

D. Symbolic Teaching

- Mahāpajāpatī embodies **fierce compassion, perseverance, and equality**.
- She is the mother of the bhikkhunī lineage — a lineage your Zen master stands in today.

4. Yasodharā — The Silent Partner in Awakening (2–3 minutes)

A. The Overlooked Story

- Siddhartha's wife, Yasodharā, is often erased in popular retellings.
- When he leaves the palace, she is not abandoned — she is already practicing.

B. Her Own Path

- She becomes an arahant.
- She raises Rāhula with dignity, not bitterness.

C. Symbolic Teaching

- Yasodharā represents **inner strength, emotional maturity, and the quiet power of letting go**.
- She shows that awakening is not only found in forests — it is found in the home, in heartbreak, in resilience.

5. Sujātā — The One Who Saved the Buddha (1–2 minutes)

A. The Offering of Milk Rice

- After years of asceticism, Siddhartha is near death.
- Sujātā, a village woman, offers him milk rice — nourishment, care, and common sense.

B. The Turning Point

- This act restores his strength and inspires the Middle Way.
- Without Sujātā, there is no Bodhi tree, no awakening.

C. Symbolic Teaching

- Sujātā embodies **the feminine wisdom of balance, nourishment, and the refusal of extremes**.

6. The Feminine in the Buddha's Awakening (2–3 minutes)

A. Māra's Daughters

- They represent seduction, distraction, and emotional turbulence.
- The Buddha does not fight them — he sees through them.

B. The Earth Witness

- When challenged by Māra, the Buddha touches the earth.
- The Earth — traditionally feminine — bears witness to his worthiness.

C. Symbolic Teaching

- The feminine here is **ground, embodiment, and truth-telling**.
- Awakening is not an escape from the world — it is a return to it.

7. The Feminine as Dharma (1–2 minutes)

Tie the threads together:

- **Māyā** — birth, mystery, embodiment
- **Mahāpajāpatī** — courage, equality, leadership
- **Yasodharā** — emotional wisdom, resilience

- **Sujātā** — nourishment, balance
- **Earth** — grounding, truth
- **Māra's daughters** — insight into desire and illusion

Teaching point: **The Buddha's life is inseparable from the feminine. The Dharma itself is inseparable from the feminine.**

8. Closing (1 minute)

- Offer a reflection: *"Awakening is not a solitary hero's journey. It is relational, embodied, and supported by countless unseen hands."*
- End with a smile-worthy line for your teacher: **"If the Buddha awakened, it is because women showed him the way."**

The Influence of the Feminine in the Life of the Buddha

We often imagine the historical Buddha as a solitary hero, achieving supreme awakening through sheer, isolated willpower in the depths of the forest. This narrative is incomplete, however, because the Buddha did not awaken in isolation. His life was deeply shaped, supported, and challenged by women at every single stage of his journey. Within the Buddhist tradition, the "feminine" represents far more than gender alone. It points toward essential qualities of the mind and heart: nurturing, intuition, relational wisdom, compassion, deep embodiment, and fierce, uncompromising clarity. By examining the women who surrounded the historical Buddha, we can trace the vital feminine principles that mapped his path to liberation.

The foundational influence begins with his mother, **Queen Māyā**, who represents the mystery of emergence and the creative force of life. Her story is steeped in rich symbolism. She dreams of a sacred white elephant entering her side, she gives birth standing up while holding a tree branch, and she passes away a mere seven days later. This beginning sends a powerful signal to practitioners: awakening is grounded, embodied, and rooted in a mother's immense courage and sacrifice. Queen Māyā's early death also introduces the young prince to the reality of profound loss, ensuring his spiritual path starts with a deeply human experience.

Following his mother's passing, **Mahāpajāpatī Gotamī**—the Buddha's aunt and stepmother—steps forward to raise him. She provides the future Buddha with his very first experience of maternal compassion. Years later, after his awakening, Mahāpajāpatī becomes the world's first feminist in the spiritual community. When she requests the ordination of women, the Buddha initially refuses, bound by the heavy patriarchal customs of ancient Indian society. Mahāpajāpatī rejects this limitation, leading five hundred women on a grueling, barefoot trek to Vesālī. They shave their heads, don saffron robes, and stand resolutely at the gates of the monastery. This fierce persistence moves Ānanda to advocate on their behalf, prompting the Buddha to relent and explicitly recognize that women are fully capable of achieving the highest fruits of enlightenment. Mahāpajāpatī embodies leadership, equality, and the mother of a lineage that stretches down to our Zen practice today.

While popular retellings often erase Siddhartha's wife, **Yasodharā**, her role is essential to his transformation. She is often cast as the abandoned victim, yet the texts reveal a woman of extraordinary resilience and independent spiritual practice. While Siddhartha searches in the forest, Yasodharā leads a life of quiet renunciation within the palace walls, eventually becoming an fully awakened *arahant* herself. She raises their son, Rāhula, with dignity rather than bitterness. Yasodharā represents emotional maturity, inner strength, and the quiet power of letting go, proving that awakening is found just as deeply in heartbreak and the home as it is in a forest hermitage.

The Archetypes of the Path

The spiritual journey of the Buddha relies on a network of feminine forces, each offering a distinct medicine:

- **Nourishment and Balance:** Sujātā prevents the Buddha's death by offering milk rice, revealing the Middle Way.
- **Insight and Clarity:** Māra's daughters test his resolve, teaching him to see through illusion without conflict.
- **Ground and Witness:** The Earth Goddess answers his touch, validating his right to sit beneath the Bodhi tree.

The turning point of the Buddha's entire ascetic trial rests in the hands of a simple village woman named **Sujātā**. After six years of extreme fasting, Siddhartha is skeletal and near death, having realized that starvation leads only to a dull mind. Sujātā observes his distress and offers him a bowl of sweet milk rice, an act of common sense, care, and basic human nourishment. This vital meal restores his physical strength, inspiring his discovery of the Middle Way between indulgence and self-mortification.

Without Sujātā's timely intervention, there is no sitting under the Bodhi tree, and there is no Buddha.

Even the climax of his awakening is explicitly relational and embodied. Sitting beneath the tree, Siddhartha faces the psychological assaults of Māra, who sends his daughters to personify seduction, desire, and emotional turbulence. The Buddha does not fight these forces; he simply witnesses them clearly until they dissolve. When Māra demands to know who will vouch for his worthiness to awaken, the Buddha does not look to a distant, celestial sky. He reaches down and touches the ground, calling upon the Earth—traditionally personified as a goddess—to bear witness to his lifetimes of practice. The Earth answers with a thundering roar of validation. Awakening, therefore, is not a flight from our world; it is a total return to the physical ground of reality.

Every thread of the Dharma is interwoven with these qualities. We see embodiment in Māyā, leadership in Mahāpajāpatī, emotional wisdom in Yasodharā, balance in Sujātā, and unshakable truth in the Earth itself. The Buddha's life is entirely inseparable from the feminine.

Our own awakening is never a solitary, heroic climb to a peak. It is a relational, embodied journey supported by countless unseen hands, ancestral lines, and everyday moments of care. If the Buddha awakened under that tree, it is because women showed him the way.

Dharma Talk Outline: Five Great Bodhisattvas and the Qualities We Are Called to Embody

1. Opening Frame (1–2 minutes)
- Introduce Bodhisattvas as **archetypes of awakened qualities**, not supernatural beings.
- Emphasize: **"These figures are mirrors. They show us what awakening looks like in human form."**
- The five most influential in Mahāyāna and Zen:
    1. Avalokiteśvara (Kannon / Guanyin)
    2. Mañjuśrī
    3. Samantabhadra
    4. Kṣitigarbha (Jizō)
    5. Maitreya

Each represents a facet of the awakened heart-mind.

2. Avalokiteśvara — Bodhisattva of Compassion (2–3 minutes)
Symbolism
- Often depicted with **1000 arms** and **eyes in each palm** — seeing suffering clearly and responding skillfully.
- In East Asia, Avalokiteśvara becomes **feminine** (Kannon/Guanyin), symbolizing compassion as a nurturing, boundless force.

Traits to Emulate
- Deep listening
- Empathy without overwhelm
- Responding to suffering with presence, not fixing
- The courage to stay open

Teaching Point

Compassion is not sentimentality — it's the willingness to be touched by the world.

3. Mañjuśrī — Bodhisattva of Wisdom (2–3 minutes)
Symbolism
- Holds a **flaming sword** that cuts through delusion.
- Holds a **lotus with a sutra** — wisdom rooted in clarity, not dogma.

- Often depicted as eternally youthful — wisdom is fresh, not rigid.

Traits to Emulate
- Discernment
- Seeing through stories and projections
- Courage to cut through self-deception
- Humor — true wisdom is light, not heavy

Teaching Point

Wisdom is not knowing more — it's believing less.

4. Samantabhadra — Bodhisattva of Action (2–3 minutes)

Symbolism
- Rides a **six-tusked white elephant** — steady, unstoppable, grounded.
- Represents vows, practice, and the embodiment of insight.

Traits to Emulate
- Taking compassionate action
- Following through on vows
- Turning insight into behavior
- Practicing with consistency, not perfection

Teaching Point

Compassion + wisdom mean nothing without action.

5. Kṣitigarbha — Bodhisattva of Vows and the Underworld (2–3 minutes)

Symbolism
- Vows not to enter Buddhahood until **all hell realms are emptied**.
- Appears as a **humble monk** with a staff and a wish-fulfilling jewel.
- Protector of children, travelers, and those in transition.

Traits to Emulate
- Fearlessness in the face of suffering
- Steadfastness
- Meeting people where they are
- Holding hope for others when they cannot hold it for themselves

Teaching Point

Ksitigarbha teaches us to walk into the darkest places with a light in our hands.

6. Maitreya — The Future Buddha (2–3 minutes)
Symbolism
- The Buddha-to-come, waiting in Tuṣita Heaven.
- Often depicted relaxed, smiling, open — the embodiment of possibility.
- Represents the **potential for awakening in every being**.

Traits to Emulate
- Patience
- Optimism grounded in practice
- Trust in the unfolding of the path
- Seeing Buddha-nature in everyone

Teaching Point
Maitreya reminds us that awakening is not behind us — it is ahead of us, in every moment.

7. Closing (1 minute)
- Summarize the five qualities:
  - **Compassion** (Avalokiteśvara)
  - **Wisdom** (Mañjuśrī)
  - **Action** (Samantabhadra)
  - **Courageous Vow** (Kṣitigarbha)
  - **Hope and Potential** (Maitreya)
- End with a unifying line: **"The Bodhisattvas are not beings we worship — they are qualities we practice."**

Five Great Bodhisattvas: Mirrors of the Awakened Heart

In the Mahāyāna and Zen traditions, Bodhisattvas are frequently encountered in liturgy and art, yet they are easily mistaken for remote, supernatural deities. In our practice, we reframe these figures entirely as psychological archetypes. They are mirrors reflecting our own innate capacity for freedom, showing us precisely what awakening looks like in an embodied human form. Five specific Bodhisattvas anchor the Zen tradition, each representing a unique, vital facet of an integrated heart-mind.

The first archetype is **Avalokiteśvara**, known as Kannon in Japan or Guanyin in China, who embodies boundless compassion. Iconography often depicts this figure with a thousand arms, featuring an open eye in the palm of each hand. This striking image symbolizes the capacity to see suffering clearly across the world and respond with appropriate skill. In East Asia, Avalokiteśvara transformed into a distinctly feminine form, emphasizing compassion as a nurturing, unconditional force. To emulate this Bodhisattva, we practice deep listening and empathy without becoming overwhelmed, learning to meet distress with absolute presence rather than a frantic urge to fix. True compassion is never sweet sentimentality; it is the raw willingness to be touched by the world.

Directly balancing compassion is **Mañjuśrī**, the Bodhisattva of transcendent wisdom. He is traditionally depicted as an eternally youthful prince riding a lion, holding a flaming sword in his right hand and a lotus supporting a sutra in his left. The sword cuts cleanly through the thick vines of our conceptual delusion, while the lotus reveals a wisdom rooted in direct clarity rather than rigid dogma. His perpetual youth reminds us that true wisdom is fresh, vibrant, and light, completely free from the heavy gravity of pedantic intellectualism. We practice as Mañjuśrī by cultivating sharp discernment, cutting through our personal projections, and maintaining a healthy sense of humor. Wisdom is not about accumulating more spiritual information; it is simply about believing our thoughts less.

Insight and compassion remain inert, however, without the grounding energy of **Samantabhadra**, the Bodhisattva of action. He is depicted riding a massive, six-tusked white elephant, an animal that moves through the world with steady, unstoppable, and dignified weight. Samantabhadra represents our vows, our actual behavior, and the physical realization of our insights. We emulate his qualities by turning our quiet meditation insights into concrete everyday behaviors, practicing with steady consistency rather than chasing an idealized notion of perfection. Wisdom and compassion mean absolutely nothing until they find expression through our hands and feet.

The Bodhisattva Mandala

Rather than separate individuals, these figures form an integrated psychological matrix within our own consciousness:

- **Avalokiteśvara:** Opens the heart to feel the world's pain.
- **Mañjuśrī:** Sharpens the mind to see through the illusion of separation.
- **Samantabhadra:** Moves the body to act skillfully on behalf of others.

When the world grows exceptionally dark, we call upon the energy of **Kṣitigarbha**, known affectionately in Japan as Jizō. He has taken a radical vow never to enter supreme Buddhahood until every single being is emptied from the hell realms. Appearing simply as a humble, barefoot monk carrying a traveler's staff and a wish-fulfilling jewel, Jizō serves as the protector of children, travelers, and those navigating difficult life transitions. We embody the spirit of Jizō when we walk fearlessly into places of deep suffering, remaining steadfast alongside those who are struggling. He teaches us how to hold hope for others when they are entirely unable to hold it for themselves, showing us how to enter the dark with a steady light in our hands.

The final figure is **Maitreya**, celebrated as the Buddha-to-come, who currently waits in the celestial realms. Unlike the other formal archetypes, Maitreya is often depicted as a relaxed, smiling, and spacious presence, completely open to the universe. He represents the sheer potential for awakening residing within every single sentient being. To practice as Maitreya, we cultivate deep patience, a radical optimism grounded in our daily practice, and an unshakeable trust in the unfolding of the path. He reminds us that realization is never a historical artifact locked in the past; it is an immediate possibility waiting for us in the very next breath.

These five figures map out our own spiritual potential. Avalokiteśvara offers us compassion, Mañjuśrī sharpens our wisdom, Samantabhadra drives our action, Kṣitigarbha grounds our courageous vows, and Maitreya fuels our ultimate hope. These Bodhisattvas are not external beings we are called to worship from afar. They are the exact qualities we are called to practice, cultivate, and embody in our lives right now.

Dharma Talk Outline: How to Cultivate Bodhicitta

1. Opening Frame (1–2 minutes)

- Start with the simplest definition: **Bodhicitta = the awakened heart-mind that seeks liberation for all beings.**
- Two aspects:
    - **Relative Bodhicitta** — compassion, empathy, the wish to help.
    - **Absolute Bodhicitta** — insight into emptiness, non-separation.
- Emphasize: **Bodhicitta is not something we manufacture. It's something we uncover.**

2. Why Bodhicitta Matters (1–2 minutes)

- Without Bodhicitta, practice becomes self-improvement.
- With Bodhicitta, practice becomes liberation for all beings.
- It transforms:
    - Meditation into compassion
    - Wisdom into service
    - Suffering into connection
- Teaching point: **Bodhicitta is the bridge between emptiness and love.**

3. The Two Types of Bodhicitta (2–3 minutes)

A. Relative Bodhicitta — The Heart That Trembles
- The natural response to suffering.
- Qualities:
    - Empathy
    - Kindness
    - Patience
    - The wish to help
- Symbol: Avalokiteśvara (Kannon) — compassion with a thousand arms.

B. Absolute Bodhicitta — The Heart That Sees Clearly

- Insight into emptiness, interdependence, non-self.
- When we see there is no separate self, compassion flows naturally.
- Symbol: Mañjuśrī — the sword that cuts through illusion.

Teaching point: **Relative Bodhicitta feels; Absolute Bodhicitta understands. Together, they liberate.**

4. The Three Classic Methods for Cultivating Bodhicitta (4–5 minutes)

1. *Recognizing Our Shared Humanity*
- Everyone wants happiness.
- Everyone fears loss.
- Everyone suffers.
- This recognition softens the heart.
- Practice: *"Just like me, this person wants to be safe. Just like me, they struggle."*

2. *Tonglen — Giving and Receiving*
- Breathe in suffering, breathe out relief.
- Not magical — psychological.
- It reverses the habit of self-protection.
- It trains the heart to stay open in the face of pain.
- Teaching point: **Tonglen transforms fear into courage, and isolation into connection.**

3. *Exchanging Self and Other (Lojong)*
- A radical shift: *"What if I cared for others the way I care for myself?"*
- Not self-neglect — self-expansion.
- It dissolves the illusion of separation.
- Practice:
    - Notice self-centered thoughts.
    - Flip the perspective.
    - Act from the larger view.

5. Obstacles to Bodhicitta (2–3 minutes)
Naming these helps people relax.

A. Self-absorption

The mind's default setting.

B. Fear of being overwhelmed

Compassion fatigue is real — but Bodhicitta is not pity.

C. Cynicism

The belief that people don't change.

D. Perfectionism

Thinking we must be saints to practice Bodhicitta.
Teaching point: **Bodhicitta grows in imperfect people — that's the whole point.**

6. Everyday Practices to Grow Bodhicitta (2–3 minutes)

A. Micro-acts of kindness

Hold a door. Let someone merge. Smile. Small acts shift the heart.

B. Listening deeply

Compassion begins with attention.

C. Softening around difficult people

Not excusing — understanding. Ask: *"What pain might be behind this behavior?"*

D. Remembering interdependence

Everything you touch touches everything else.

E. Dedication of merit

End practice with: *"May this benefit all beings."* This rewires intention.

7. The Zen Expression of Bodhicitta (1–2 minutes)

A. Bodhicitta is the Bodhisattva Vow in action.

B. It's the heart of zazen: Sitting not just for yourself, but for all beings.

C. **Master Seung Sahn's Turning Phrase: "How may I help you?"**

- The ultimate answer to a conceptual koan trap (e.g., the sound of one hand, hanging from a tree by your teeth).
- Shifting instantly from *"What am I experiencing?"* to *"What does this moment require?"*

D. **It's the spirit of Jizō, Kannon, Samantabhadra — the willingness to show up, again and again, with an open heart.**

E. Teaching point: **When nothing else makes sense—be a Bodhisattva.**

8. **Closing (1 minute)**
   - Bring it home: **"Bodhicitta is not something we achieve — it's our natural heart when fear relaxes."**
   - Invite practitioners to choose one small act of Bodhicitta today.
   - End with a line that always lands: **"When one heart opens, the whole world opens."**

How to Cultivate Bodhicitta

At the core of the Mahāyāna tradition lies a profound spiritual orientation known as *bodhicitta*. Translated simplest as the awakened heart-mind, *bodhicitta* is the deep, internal aspiration to achieve liberation not just for oneself, but for the benefit of all sentient beings. This realization operates through two distinct dimensions: relative *bodhicitta*, which manifests as active compassion, empathy, and the wish to help, and absolute *bodhicitta*, which is our direct insight into emptiness and non-separation. It is essential to understand that *bodhicitta* is not a state of mind we must laboriously manufacture through willpower. It is our innate, fundamental nature, waiting to be uncovered whenever our habitual fears begin to relax.

Without this altruistic orientation, our spiritual practice easily degenerates into a sophisticated form of self-improvement, akin to going to a psychological gym just to build a stronger ego. With *bodhicitta*, however, every moment on the meditation cushion becomes an act of universal liberation. This intention transforms our formal meditation into active compassion, our intellectual wisdom into selfless service, and our personal suffering into a bridge of deep connection with others. It serves as the irreplaceable link connecting the profound realization of emptiness with the expression of unconditional love.

To cultivate this quality effectively, we must look at how its two dimensions interlock. Relative *bodhicitta* can be described as the heart that trembles in the direct face of suffering, expressing itself through empathy, kindness, patience, and a protective urge to help. It is beautifully symbolized by Avalokiteśvara, the Bodhisattva of Compassion, reaching out with a thousand arms to meet the pain of the world. Absolute *bodhicitta*, conversely, is the heart that sees clearly, rooted in the sharp wisdom of Mañjuśrī. When we realize through deep insight that there is no solid, separate self to defend, compassion flows outward as naturally as sunlight. Relative *bodhicitta* feels the world's pain;

absolute *bodhicitta* understands the underlying reality. Together, they bring true liberation.

The Core Cultivation Methods

The tradition provides three classic psychological practices to systematically open the heart-mind:

- **Recognizing Shared Humanity:** Constantly reminding ourselves that every single person desires happiness, fears loss, and struggles with suffering exactly like we do.
- **Tonglen (Giving and Receiving):** A visualization practice of breathing in the raw suffering of others and breathing out relief, reversing our hardwired instinct for self-protection.
- **Exchanging Self and Other:** A radical shift in perspective where we deliberately treat the needs, fears, and joys of others with the exact same care we usually reserve for ourselves.

As we engage in this cultivation, we will inevitably encounter internal obstacles, and naming them allows us to relax without self-judgment. We experience the heavy gravity of self-absorption, which is simply the mind's defensive default setting. We encounter the fear of being emotionally overwhelmed, forgetting that true *bodhicitta* is a vast reservoir of presence rather than the draining exhaustion of pity or codependency. We hit walls of cynicism, or we fall into the trap of perfectionism, mistakenly believing we must be flawless saints before we can practice. *Bodhicitta* grows exclusively within imperfect people; that reality is the entire point of the path.

In our everyday lives, we grow this awakened heart through tiny, unassuming gestures. We practice through micro-acts of kindness, like holding a door, letting a car merge in traffic, or offering a genuine smile, letting these small choices shift our inner momentum. We practice by listening deeply, understanding that true compassion always begins with unhurried attention. When dealing with difficult individuals, we choose to soften, looking past the abrasive surface behavior to ask what hidden pain might be driving their actions. We maintain an awareness of our deep interdependence, remembering that everything we touch touches the entire web of existence.

In the Zen tradition, this altruistic orientation is expressed directly through our dedication of merit at the end of every practice session, offering our efforts with the vow: *"May this benefit all beings."* We sit in zazen not to achieve a private escape from our problems, but to steady ourselves on behalf of the entire world.

To bring this training into its sharpest, most immediate focus, the Korean Zen tradition relies on a legendary turning phrase from Zen Master Seung Sahn. When his students would become hopelessly entangled in the dense, conceptual traps of koan interviews—struggling to demonstrate the sound of one hand or facing the existential paralysis of hanging from a cliffside tree branch by their teeth—Seung Sahn would pierce through the intellectual fog with a simple, arresting question: **"How may I help you?"**

This question is the ultimate distillation of absolute and relative *bodhicitta* combined. It functions as a psychological circuit breaker. The moment we ask *"How may I help you?"*, the heavy, protective architecture of the separate ego instantly collapses. We stop asking, *"How do I feel? Am I succeeding? Am I enlightened?"* and instead ask, *"What does this immediate situation require of me?"* The entire universe transforms from a threat to be managed into a relationship to be served.

When the world grows chaotic, when our personal conditioning flares, or when our formal meditation insights feel dry and distant, this phrase serves as our absolute compass. When nothing else seems to make sense, the instruction is clear: **Be a Bodhisattva.** Step forward into your don't-know mind, drop the scoreboard of your spiritual progress, and simply ask the world around you how you may serve it.

Bodhicitta is not a distant trophy to win; it is the natural warmth of our own heart whenever we allow our defenses to drop. By choosing just one small act of open-hearted presence today, we realize a beautiful truth: when one single heart opens, the whole world opens along with it.

Dharma Talk Outline: The Four Great Bodhisattva Vows — The Heart of the Zen Path

1. Opening Frame (1–2 minutes)

Begin with the centrality of the vows in Zen practice: **"These vows are impossible — and we take them anyway."**

Emphasize that the vows are not commandments or goals. They are **orientations, aspirations,** and **expressions of awakening**.

Teaching point: **The vows describe the awakened heart — and they also create it.**

2. The First Vow: Sentient Beings Are Numberless; We Vow to Save Them All (3–4 minutes)

A. The Paradox

There are infinite beings. We cannot possibly save them all. And yet we vow to.

B. What "Saving" Really Means

Not rescuing. Not fixing. Not converting. Saving means **meeting suffering with presence and compassion**.

C. The Zen Angle

Every moment is a sentient being: a thought, a feeling, a person, a situation.

D. Practice Pointer

"How can I help right now?" Not in theory — in this moment.

3. The Second Vow: Delusions Are Endless; We Vow to Cut Through Them All (3–4 minutes)

A. Endless Delusions

Thoughts, stories, habits, fears, identities — they never stop arising.

B. Cutting Through

Not suppressing. Not fighting. Cutting through means **seeing clearly**.

C. The Zen Angle

Delusion is not the enemy. Delusion is the **raw material** of awakening.

D. Practice Pointer

Notice the story. Return to the breath. Cut through by seeing.

4. The Third Vow: The Teachings Are Infinite; We Vow to Learn Them All (3–4 minutes)

A. Infinite Teachings: The word "Dharma Gates" is translated here seamlessly as teachings. It means every single encounter, condition, and environment is a lesson.

B. Learning Them All: Not academic study or memory retention, but the willingness to listen and remain an eternal student of reality.

C. The Zen Angle: True teachings are not restricted to parchment or books; they appear in the messy reality of the immediate moment.

5. The Fourth Vow: The Buddha Way Is Inconceivable; We Vow to Attain It (3–4 minutes)

A. Inconceivable: The ultimate realization cannot be captured by the conceptual brain, held in the hand, or reduced to a logical thought.

B. We Vow to Attain It: The great Zen paradox—attaining what cannot be conceived. This anchors the practice in wholehearted devotion and absolute effort, completely free from the ego's desire to "own" enlightenment.

6. The Vows as a Whole (2–3 minutes)

Show how the vows interpenetrate:
Saving beings is compassion.
Cutting delusions is wisdom.
Entering Dharma gates is mindfulness.
Embodying the Buddha Way is the integration of all three.
Teaching point: The vows are not four — they are one vow seen from four angles.

7. The Impossible Vows and the Zen Spirit (2–3 minutes)

Highlight the paradox:
We vow to do what cannot be done.
We vow to finish what cannot be finished.
We vow to awaken to what cannot be grasped.
This is the Bodhisattva spirit — infinite commitment, infinite compassion, infinite humility.
Zen expression: "We take the vows not because we can fulfill them, but because they are true."

8. Practical Application (2 minutes)

Invite practitioners to reflect:
Which vow is alive for you right now?
Which vow challenges you?
Which vow comforts you?
Which vow calls you forward?
Offer a simple practice: Choose one vow to carry through your day.

9. Closing (1 minute)

End with the essential reminder: **The vows are not about perfection — they are about direction. They point us toward the awakened heart.**

Encourage practitioners to chant the vows not as promises, but as **expressions of their deepest intention.**

The Four Great Bodhisattva Vows: The Heart of the Zen Path

In Zen temples across the world, practitioners chant the Four Great Bodhisattva Vows at the conclusion of every formal meditation period. In our lineage, passed down through Zen Master Seung Sahn, these vows present an immediate, staggering paradox that defines the entire spirit of our tradition: *"These vows are completely impossible—and we take them anyway."* To an analytical mind driven by goals and milestones, promising to achieve the unachievable sounds entirely absurd. Within the Zen framework, however, the vows are neither moral commandments to follow nor distant targets to cross off a list. They are orientations of the mind, continuous aspirations, and the direct, operational expressions of an awakened life.

The path opens with the first radical commitment: **"Sentient beings are numberless; we vow to save them all."** The paradox here is absolute, because the suffering of our world is vast, endless, and entirely beyond our solitary capacity to eradicate. Yet, the vow remains unshaken. In our practice, we reframe what it means to "save" another being. It has nothing to do with heroic rescuing, codependent fixing, or religious conversion. Saving another simply means meeting their suffering with complete, unhurried presence and fierce compassion. Looked at through the micro-lens of Zen, every single passing moment is a sentient being. A difficult thought, a painful physical sensation, a heavy emotion, or an irritating encounter—each of these is a fleeting form of life arising in our awareness. We practice with this immense vow by distilling it into a simple, immediate internal inquiry: *"How can I help right now?"* We do not worry about saving the planet in theory; we show up fully for the specific situation unfolding right in front of us.

Having oriented our heart toward others, the second vow turns our attention inward to the nature of mind: **"Delusions are**

endless; we vow to cut through them all." Thoughts, anxieties, manufactured stories, old habits, and rigid identities arise unceasingly throughout our day. Cutting through this endless parade does not mean aggressively suppressing our thoughts or waging an internal war against our psychology. True cutting means seeing clearly. In Zen, we discover that delusion is never an enemy to be destroyed; it is the raw material of our awakening. Just as mud is indispensable for the blooming of a lotus, our delusions are the exact places where wisdom reveals itself. We apply this vow practically by noticing when the mind spins a dramatic personal story, anchoring ourselves firmly back in the breath, and dissolving the illusion simply by refusing to look away from its empty nature.

This clarity prepares us to face the outer world once more through the lens of the third commitment: **"The teachings are infinite; we vow to learn them all."** Traditional translations often refer to "Dharma gates," but framing them as *infinite teachings* brings a vital, immediate accessibility to our daily lives. A teaching is any environment or condition through which the truth of reality reveals itself. Every sudden change in our plans, every unexpected grief, every joy, and every minor daily irritation is an infinite classroom. To "learn them all" does not imply an academic race to memorize scriptures or accumulate spiritual credentials. Instead, it demands a posture of ultimate humility—the willingness to remain a beginner, to listen deeply to our lives, and to meet each unique circumstance without our armor of certainty. The authentic Dharma is never locked away inside leather-bound books; it is alive in the messy context of our relationships, our careers, and our heartbreaks.

The final vow brings us face-to-face with the ultimate nature of Zen training: **"The Buddha way is inconceivable; we vow to attain it."** This is the ultimate expression of infinite practice, a path completely unburdened by a finish line. The human intellect naturally seeks to categorize, conceptualize, and possess its experiences. Yet, the true nature of reality remains completely *inconceivable*—it cannot be captured by ideas or held by the logical brain. The ego-self desperately wants to cross a finish line, claim a title, and be declared enlightened. True realization, however, means attaining what cannot be conceived, stepping off the cliff of our concepts and plunging into the absolute immediacy of *"Just this."* We fulfill this unattainable vow by resting deeply in the simplicity of our original, don't-know mind. This single breath, this immediate choice—this is where the inconceivable Buddha way is completely attained and embodied.

The Fourfold Matrix of One Vow

The Great Vows are not four separate tasks; they form a single, integrated expression of our original nature seen from four distinct angles:

- **The First Vow (Compassion)**: Directing our energy outward to meet the boundless field of suffering beings.
- **The Second Vow (Wisdom)**: Piercing through our internal illusions and defensive mental structures.
- **The Third Vow (Mindfulness)**: Stepping courageously into the infinite teachings of daily life.
- **The Fourth Vow (Integration)**: Fully embodying the inconceivable path of awakening in this very step.

When we see the vows through this integrated framework, we realize they do not describe a future state of perfection, but a real-time orientation for this very moment. Saving numberless beings, cutting through endless delusions, learning infinite teachings, and attaining an inconceivable path all happen right here and now.

This willingness to dedicate our entire life to what cannot be logically finished is the true essence of the Bodhisattva spirit. It requires an infinite commitment, an infinite compassion, and an infinite humility. A beautiful Zen expression captures this attitude perfectly: "We take the vows not because we can fulfill them, but because they are true." They give our human life a clear, unshakeable direction, completely independent of whether we achieve a perfect, final result.

We can bring these boundless vows down into our immediate day by checking which of them speaks to us most clearly right now. We can notice which vow comforts our anxiety, which one challenges our complacency, and which one urges our practice forward. By carrying just one of these four aspects through our daily routines, we transform our ordinary actions into a vehicle for universal liberation. The Four Great Vows are never a heavy promise of future perfection; they are the vibrant, immediate expression of your own awakened heart, waking up to the world in this very breath.

PART 6 - Zen and Our Modern World

Dharma Talk Outline: The Six Realms of Existence

1. Opening Frame (1–2 minutes)
- Introduce the Six Realms as **a psychological and existential map**, not a literal cosmology you must believe in.
- Emphasize: *"These realms describe states of mind we cycle through daily."*
- Connect to practice: The point is not to judge the realms but to **recognize them and wake up within them**.

2. The Six Realms (6–8 minutes total)
Present each realm as both a mythic image and a lived experience.

A. Hell Realm — Anger & Aversion
- Mythic: beings tormented by fire, cold, or conflict.
- Psychological: rage, resentment, self-hatred, the "everything is wrong" mindset.
- Practice pointer: Notice the contraction. Can I soften? Can I breathe?

B. Hungry Ghost Realm — Insatiable Craving
- Mythic: beings with huge bellies and tiny mouths.
- Psychological: addiction, compulsive scrolling, never-enoughness, emotional hunger.
- Practice pointer: What am I trying to fill? What happens if I pause before reaching?

C. Animal Realm — Habit & Fear
- Mythic: beings driven by instinct.
- Psychological: autopilot, avoidance, comfort-seeking, fear of change.
- Practice pointer: Bring curiosity to routine. One mindful breath breaks the spell.

D. Human Realm — Desire & Opportunity

- Mythic: the realm of pleasure, pain, and spiritual potential.
- Psychological: our everyday life — mixed, messy, workable.
- Practice pointer: This is the realm where awakening is possible. Don't waste it.

E. Asura Realm — Competition & Jealousy
- Mythic: warrior gods fighting endlessly.
- Psychological: comparison, insecurity, "I should be further along," spiritual one-upmanship.
- Practice pointer: Rejoice in others' success. Drop the scoreboard.

F. God Realm — Bliss & Complacency
- Mythic: beings in long-lasting pleasure who eventually fall.
- Psychological: comfort, success, spiritual bypassing, "I'm fine, no need to practice."
- Practice pointer: Remember impermanence. Comfort is not liberation.

3. The Wheel Turns (1–2 minutes)
- We move through these realms constantly — sometimes all six before breakfast.
- The realms are **not a hierarchy** but a mirror.
- The hub of the wheel is **ignorance, craving, and aversion** — the forces that keep us spinning.

4. The Way Out: The Buddha in Each Realm (2–3 minutes)
Each realm contains a Buddha offering liberation:
- Hell: cooling water — compassion.
- Hungry Ghost: nourishment — presence.
- Animal: a book — awareness.
- Human: teachings — practice.
- Asura: a mirror — self-recognition.
- God: a reminder of impermanence — humility.

Teaching point: **We don't escape the realms by force; we
wake up within them.**

5. Closing (1 minute)

- Invite practitioners to notice which realm they've
  visited today.
- Encourage gentle awareness rather than self-judgment.
- End with: *"Wherever you find yourself, the Dharma is already
  there."*

The Six Realms: Waking Up in the Midst of the Wheel

In traditional Buddhist teachings, the Six Realms of Samsara are often presented as a literal cosmology of rebirth. In our practice, however, we approach them as a profound psychological and existential map. These realms describe specific states of mind that we cycle through continually, sometimes experiencing all six before breakfast. The point of studying this map is not to judge our mental states, but to recognize them clearly so we can wake up right in the middle of them.

The journey around the wheel begins with the **Hell Realm**, powered by the forces of anger and aversion. Mythologically, this realm is depicted as a place of intense torment by fire, cold, or ceaseless conflict. Psychologically, we inhabit this realm whenever we are consumed by rage, burning resentment, self-hatred, or a rigid mindset where everything feels completely wrong. Our practice pointer in this painful state is to notice the physical contraction in the body, asking ourselves: "Can I soften? Can I breathe?"

Next is the **Hungry Ghost Realm**, driven by insatiable craving. The mythic images show beings with massive, bloated bellies but tiny, needle-thin mouths, meaning they can never take in enough nourishment to satisfy their hunger. We live this experience through addiction, compulsive phone scrolling, emotional dependency, and a chronic sense of "never-enoughness." When caught in this cycle, we must pause and ask what we are truly trying to fill, investigating the empty feeling before we reach for the next distraction.

We then encounter the **Animal Realm**, which is characterized by habit, fear, and instinct. Mythologically, it is the world of beings driven entirely by survival; psychologically, it represents our autopilot mode. We enter this realm when we seek comfort at all costs, avoid looking at our patterns, and resist change out of fear. To break this spell of dull routine, we must bring

curiosity to our habits, remembering that a single mindful breath
can disrupt a lifetime of conditioning.

The Higher Realms of the Mind

As the wheel turns, we move into the more subtle, comfortable,
or complex states of consciousness:

- **The Human Realm (Desire & Opportunity):** A
  mixed, messy landscape of pleasure and pain. This is
  the precious realm of workable experience where
  awakening is uniquely possible.
- **The Asura Realm (Competition & Jealousy):** The
  mind of the warrior gods, obsessed with comparison,
  insecurity, and spiritual one-upmanship. We practice
  here by dropping the scoreboard and rejoicing in the
  success of others.
- **The God Realm (Bliss & Complacency):** A state of
  high success, comfort, or temporary meditative bliss.
  The danger here is spiritual bypassing and a total loss
  of the urge to practice, forgetting that comfort is not
  liberation.

This constant movement through the realms is not a linear
hierarchy. The wheel is a mirror, and its central hub is driven by
ignorance, craving, and aversion. These are the three poisons
that keep the entire structure spinning.

The most beautiful insight of this teaching is that the historical
Buddha is traditionally depicted as appearing within every single
realm, offering a unique key to liberation.

- In Hell, the Buddha offers the cooling water of
  compassion.
- In the Hungry Ghost realm, he offers the true
  nourishment of **presence**.
- In the Animal realm, he holds a book, symbolizing
  awareness over instinct.

- In the Human realm, he provides the **teachings** and encouragement to practice.
- In the Asura realm, he holds a mirror, forcing **self-recognition** over comparison.
- In the God realm, he offers a reminder of **impermanence** to cut through complacency.

We do not escape these psychological realms by using brute force or by wishing our minds were different. We free ourselves simply by waking up within them. We can choose to gently notice which realm we are visiting today without a single drop of self-judgment. Wherever you happen to find yourself on the wheel, the Dharma is already there, waiting to be discovered.

Dharma Talk Outline: Mindfulness, Compassion, and Wisdom — The Threefold Path of One Dharma

1. Opening Frame (1–2 minutes)

Begin with Goldstein's teaching as a unifying principle for Western Buddhism: "The method is mindfulness, the expression is compassion, the essence is wisdom."
Emphasize that these are not three separate practices — they are three facets of one awakened mind.
Teaching point: Mindfulness reveals reality. Compassion responds to reality. Wisdom understands reality.

2. Mindfulness — The Method (3–4 minutes)

A. What Mindfulness Really Means
Not concentration, not relaxation, not self-improvement. Mindfulness is non-judgmental awareness of the present moment.

B. Why It Comes First
Without mindfulness, we don't see clearly. Without seeing clearly, compassion is sentimental and wisdom is conceptual.

C. How Mindfulness Functions in Practice
It interrupts autopilot.
It reveals feeling tone before reaction.
It shows us the Three Poisons in real time.
It grounds us in the body, breath, and senses.

D. Practice Pointer
"Just this." One breath, one sensation, one thought — known clearly.

3. Compassion — The Expression (3–4 minutes)
A. Compassion as the Natural Response to Seeing Clearly
When mindfulness shows us suffering — in ourselves or others — the heart naturally softens.

B. Compassion Is Not Sentimentality

It is not pity, not rescuing, not fixing. It is the willingness to stay present with suffering without turning away.

C. The Two Directions of Compassion

Inward: meeting our own pain with gentleness.
Outward: meeting others with patience, generosity, and care.

D. Compassion as a Bodhisattva Expression

When mindfulness opens the door, compassion walks through it.

E. Practice Pointer

"May this suffering be held in kindness."

4. Wisdom — The Essence (3–4 minutes)

A. Wisdom Is Not Intellectual

It is not knowledge, philosophy, or belief. Wisdom is direct insight into the nature of reality.

B. What Wisdom Sees

Impermanence
Non-self
Interdependence
Emptiness
The constructed nature of experience

C. How Wisdom Frees Us

When we see that everything is changing, we stop clinging. When we see that nothing is separate, compassion deepens. When we see that the self is a process, suffering loosens.

D. Wisdom as the Flower of Mindfulness and Compassion

Mindfulness reveals the truth. Compassion opens the heart to the truth. Wisdom understands the truth.

E. Practice Pointer

"Not two." No separation between self and other, form and emptiness, practice and life.

5. The Three as One Path (2–3 minutes)
Show how they interpenetrate:
Mindfulness without compassion becomes dry.
Compassion without wisdom becomes overwhelmed.
Wisdom without mindfulness becomes abstract.
Together, they form a complete path.
Zen expression: "Clear seeing, open heart, liberated action."

6. Practical Application (2 minutes)
Invite practitioners to reflect:
Where is mindfulness alive in my life?
Where is compassion needed right now?
Where is wisdom quietly showing itself?

Offer a simple daily practice: **Pause → Notice → Soften → Understand.**

7. Closing (1 minute)

End with Goldstein's line again, now embodied: **"The method is mindfulness, the expression is compassion, the essence is wisdom."**

Invite practitioners to let these three qualities guide one moment of their day — one breath, one interaction, one choice.

Mindfulness, Compassion, and Wisdom: The Threefold Path of One Dharma

Contemporary Buddhist practice is beautifully illuminated by an insightful summary from the teacher Joseph Goldstein: *"The method is mindfulness, the expression is compassion, the essence is wisdom."* This teaching offers a powerful unifying principle for our spiritual journey. Rather than pointing toward three distinct, isolated practices to be checked off a list, these three qualities represent three facets of a single, integrated, awakened mind. They work together in absolute harmony. Mindfulness reveals reality exactly as it is, compassion responds to reality with an open heart, and wisdom understands reality at its deepest level.

To navigate this unified path, we begin with **Mindfulness**, which serves as our primary method. Mindfulness is frequently romanticized in modern culture as a trendy relaxation technique or a vehicle for self-improvement, but its true function is far more radical. It is the non-judgmental, bare awareness of the present moment. This quality must come first because without it, we simply do not see our lives clearly. Without clear vision, our compassion inevitably degenerates into sticky sentimentality, and our wisdom becomes a collection of dry, intellectual concepts. In our everyday lives, mindfulness acts as a circuit breaker for our conditioning. It interrupts our robotic autopilot, reveals our hidden emotional reactions before they explode, and grounds us firmly in the physical reality of the body, the breath, and the senses. We practice this method by resting in the simplicity of a two-word pointer: *"Just this."* One breath, one physical sensation, or one passing thought, known clearly exactly as it occurs.

When mindfulness shines its light into the dark corners of our experience, it naturally gives birth to **Compassion**, the outward expression of the path. When clear awareness exposes the reality of suffering—whether that pain lives inside our own hearts or in the lives of those around us—the heart-mind naturally softens. True compassion is completely free from the heavy gravity of sentimentality, pity, or a frantic, codependent urge to rescue and fix. It is, quite simply, the courageous willingness to stay present with suffering without turning our faces away. This quality flows in two vital directions: inward, meeting our personal failures and wounds with radical gentleness, and outward, meeting a chaotic world with patience, generosity, and care. When mindfulness opens the doorway of the present moment, compassion is the force that steps through it. We cultivate this expression by holding our difficulties in a quiet, internal phrase: *"May this suffering be held in kindness."*

The Danger of Isolation

These three facets are deeply co-dependent, and separating them cripples our spiritual development:

- **Mindfulness without compassion** becomes cold, detached, clinical, and dry.
- **Compassion without wisdom** lacks boundary and insight, leading directly to becoming overwhelmed and exhausted by burnout.
- **Wisdom without mindfulness** loses its footing in lived experience, evaporating into abstract philosophy and empty dogma.

The ultimate maturity of this practice culminates in **Wisdom**, the very essence of the Dharma. Wisdom is never an intellectual accumulation of information, scholarship, or philosophical belief. It is the direct, non-conceptual insight into the true nature of reality. Wisdom looks at the world and sees the truths of impermanence, non-self, interdependence, and emptiness. It witnesses the completely constructed, fleeting nature of our daily experience. This seeing is what radically frees us from our psychological bondage. When we see that everything is changing, our desperate habit of clinging dissolves. When we recognize that nothing exists as a separate entity, our compassion deepens into a universal force. When we see that the ego-self is a fluid process rather than a solid monument, our suffering finally loosens its grip. Wisdom is the beautiful flower that blooms from the soil of mindfulness and the water of compassion. Its ultimate practice pointer is found in the classic phrase: *"Not two."* There is no final separation between self and other, form and emptiness, or meditation practice and everyday life.

Together, these three qualities form a complete, unshakeable path of liberation. The Zen tradition expresses this elegant alignment through a simple formula: *"Clear seeing, open heart, liberated action."* We do not need to wait for a special, future retreat to embody this teaching; we can apply it to our lives in real-time through a simple four-step sequence: Pause, Notice, Soften, and Understand.

We can pause at any moment today and check the alignment of our own heart-mind, asking ourselves: Where is mindfulness alive in my life right now? Where is compassion needed in this very encounter? Where is wisdom quietly showing itself beneath the noise? By anchoring ourselves in Goldstein's guiding principle, we allow mindfulness, compassion, and wisdom to direct a single breath, a single choice, or a single interaction. When we train our minds in this way, we discover that the path is not a distant destination; it is the very way we walk through our world.

Epilogue: Returning to the Source

As this collection of Dharma reflections comes to a close, we return to the simple truth that has quietly threaded itself through every page: the Dharma is not somewhere else. It is not hidden in distant scriptures, locked in ancient languages, or reserved for monasteries on faraway mountains. It is here — in the breath you are taking now, in the sensations of your body, in the joys and frictions of your relationships, in the unguarded moments when your heart opens without effort.

Throughout these talks, we have walked through the landscapes of the Six Realms, the machinery of the senses, the spirals of karma, the vastness of emptiness, the vows of the Bodhisattva, and the luminous simplicity of don't-know mind. Each teaching points to a different facet of the same jewel. Each one invites us to look directly at our experience and discover that awakening is not an event, but a way of meeting the world.

If there is a single thread that binds these teachings together, it is this: **the path is lived in the middle of our ordinary lives**. The Buddha awakened under a tree, but he lived his awakening on dusty roads, in crowded marketplaces, in conversations with kings and beggars, in moments of conflict and moments of tenderness. Our own practice unfolds in the same terrain — in the kitchen, in the workplace, in the quiet hours of the night, in the unexpected places where suffering and compassion meet.

The Dharma does not ask us to become someone else. It asks us to become intimate with who we already are.

It asks us to see clearly.

To respond with compassion.

To act with integrity.

To rest in the spaciousness that appears when we stop clinging to our stories.

To trust that even in confusion, even in fear, even in the midst of the spinning wheel of samsara, there is a place within us that is steady, awake, and unbroken.

If these talks have offered even one moment of clarity, one breath of relief, one shift toward kindness — then they have done their work. If they have raised new questions, stirred new uncertainties, or revealed new layers of delusion — then they have also done their work. The Dharma is not meant to close things down. It is meant to open them.

As you continue your practice — in the zendo, on Zoom, in your sangha, in the quiet corners of your life — may these teachings serve as companions rather than conclusions. May they remind you that the path is not linear, that awakening is not a finish line, and that every moment is a fresh invitation to begin again.

Wherever you find yourself — in joy or sorrow, clarity or confusion, stillness or chaos — the Dharma is already there, waiting patiently for you to notice.

Only go straight.

Only don't know.

Trust that the way reveals itself with every step.

ONE DHARMA ZEN
Mindfulness - Compassion - Wisdom

www.ingramcontent.com/pod-product-compliance
Lightning Source LLC
Chambersburg PA
CBHW020543160726
47991CB00002B/558